Lifting the Veil

Lifting the Veil
Practical Kabbalah
with Kundalini Yoga

THE EXPANDED AND REVISED WORK

ROOTLIGHT, INC.
NEW YORK, NY

Also by Joseph Michael Levry (Gurunam):

Alchemy of Love Relationships

The Splendor of the Sun

Regarding the name Gurunam:

Gurunam is a spiritual name given to me by Yogi Bhajan, master of White Tantric and Kundalini yoga. "Gu" stands for darkness or duality and "ru" stands for light or divinity. "Nam" means the power of the spoken word or sound.

"In principio erat verbum et verbum erat a pud Deum, et Deus erat verbum. In the beginning was the Word and the Word was with God and the Word was God." The name Gurunam represents a person who uses the power of the word or sound to bring light into people's lives.

Rootlight, Inc.
15 Park Avenue, Suite 7C
New York, NY 10016

CREDITS:

Design: *Renée Skuba*

Inside Photography: *Pauline St. Denis, Fredric Reshew*

Models: *Nidhi Adhiya, Noemie Ditzler, Ken Dubois,*
Alyssa Gaustad, Primavera Salva, Kim Ulrich

Printed in the United States of America
For Worldwide Distribution
ISBN 1-885562-02-0
Library of Congress # 2002096636

Printed on recycled paper.

Contents

Acknowledgments

This book is dedicated with boundless love to my mother for showing me the way of sharing; to my sisters for teaching me the art of grace; to my brothers and beloved uncle for their unshakeable support; and to my late father to whom I owe this path.

Thank you to Yogi Bhajan for teaching me the invaluable science of Kundalini yoga.

Many thanks to Hortense Dodo, Ph.D., Gururattan Kaur Khalsa, Ph.D., Jonathan Terner, the Harkeys, Sabra Petersmann, Renée Skuba, Deborah Joyce, plus many others for their assistance, input and undying support of this work.

Once again, I want to extend my deepest gratitude to all those who have helped me organize, edit and produce *Lifting the Veil*. Without their labors of love, this would not have come together with such ease.

Preface

This enlarged and revised version of *Lifting the Veil* is a response to the many dedicated readers who have asked for more; who have shown interest in delving deeper; who long to go further into the principles and practices of the sacred sciences of Kabbalah and Kundalini yoga. Those genuine desires, coupled with the challenges currently facing humans on planet earth, prompted me to expand the information contained in the first edition.

Although this revised edition of *Lifting the Veil* contains the foundation of the first book, readers will find much more new material. I have included esoteric information previously kept hidden from the lay population as well as more advanced meditations. I reveal these priceless teachings to you with hope and prayer that you will take them and share them with others, for this priceless information is meant for everyone. It is the birthright of each and every human to possess. By learning this timeless wisdom and serving humankind with it, you will be attuned to and blessed by the heavenly hierarchies, for heaven always serves those who serve others. Now is the time to learn these teachings and serve humankind.

Very soon, more and more people will be teaching and talking about the depth and efficacy of the truths contained in this book. Direct everyone to these teachings and use them for yourself. They will take away your fears, and empower you to reach your goals while at the same time helping others to reach theirs. These teachings will expand your consciousness, purify your mind, and illuminate your life. They will show you how to cause heaven to shower you with blessings.

The information contained within *Lifting the Veil* is a missing link; learning it will give you a solid spiritual foundation for understanding the essence of the holy Kabbalah and its application to specific problems. This book will help you understand and clarify the confusion about the Kabbalah and other spiritual systems. In addition, it reveals profound meditations that you can practice to accelerate your spiritual growth, heal yourself and uplift others.

Ordinarily the reader of the divine spiritual wisdom or arcane work must have the esoteric keys in order to penetrate the heart of the work. There are keys hidden within this book and the more often you read *Lifting the Veil*, the more doors of spiritual wisdom can you unlock. What you receive and what is revealed is based upon your level of consciousness. The more you read *Lifting the Veil* the more you will get out of it.

Working with this sacred science will open up a whole new life for you and release new energies, which have been hidden deep within you waiting to unfold. *Lifting the Veil* is the missing link which will help you find yourself. For you will never find God until you find yourself. This wisdom will become a source of infinite power and wonderful blessings.

This book is for all yogis, Kabbalists, doctors, serious health practitioners and everyone who desires to walk the distance from the head to the heart, so as contribute to a positive evolution of the human race. It is important that each person, like yourself, who walks the path of light, transforms themselves into a bright ray of the Sun. As agents of light, we are instrumental in ensuring that the Sun of wisdom, strength, and beauty shines ever more brightly right here and now throughout our daily lives.

Introducing
Joseph Michael Levry (Gurunam)
by Gururattan Kaur Khalsa, Ph.D.

That Joseph Michael Levry (Gurunam) is an exceptional human being is evident in his presence that openly emanates love for all to partake. His tireless commitment to the elevation of the consciousness of the planet is remarkable. Beyond his personal charisma and dedication to spreading light to all human beings he is an unmatched scholar and teacher. There are several points that make Gurunam's work not only unique, but destined to play a pivotal role in transforming the planet.

In his book *Lifting the Veil*, he freely shares the heretofore kept secrets of two ancient sciences and removes the mystery of Kabbalah. The essence of Kabbalah is the revelation of how the Universe works and how it impacts human life. Gurunam has decoded the essence of Kabbalah from the previously embroidered language that perpetuated confusion and separation from the Source. Gurunam presents it in a form that is simultaneously powerful and easy to understand. Gurunam offers Kabbalah as a practical and simple science that can be applied to everyday life. He explains in simple language:

- *How the Universe works and how to live according to the laws*
- *The process by which people get sick and how it can be reversed*
- *How to remove the shadow and negativity that create disease and suffering*
- *How to remove the negativity in the mind*
- *How to create and hold a space for healing*

He breaks down the myth of healing and delineates the complete process. He explains what is actually taking place so that people know what they are doing and why and how to create change. His work transcends the theology that separates humans from the Divine, from each other and themselves. It is ecumenical. Gurunam accurately explains the historical development of Kabbalah and how it evolved from Egyptian times and was incorporated into Judaism and Christianity.

For the first time in the history of humankind, Gurunam has integrated the two sciences of Kundalini yoga and Kabbalah. He has even been praised by the Master of Kundalini Yoga Yogi Bhajan for this awesome contribution.

Gururattan Kaur Khalsa, Ph.D. *(University of Geneva, Switzerland), taught at MIT, Stanford University, Dartmouth College, New Hampshire College, U.S. International University (San Diego), Institute of Transpersonal Psychology (Palo Alto). Author of six Kundalini yoga and meditation manuals,* Inner and Outer Ecology, Your Life is in Your Chakras, The Destiny of Women is the Destiny of the World, *and* Love IT with All Your Heart.

Introduction

Why let time and circumstance shape the course of your life? Why be affected by fate? Within and all around you are natural principles and definite laws, which can be learned, applied and mastered. Kabbalists and yogis have long known that life is not a matter of chance, but that for each action there is a cause and a reaction. Thus, the things we desire most—being happy, healthy and loved—are personal choices based on the understanding and application of certain natural principles. Until recently, this science had never been revealed to anyone outside a small circle. Now more than ever, is the time in which greater truths regarding the salvation of humankind at this present moment in history are being brought forward in order to bring about a healing metamorphosis of present society. The cause of the actual world crisis comes from human ignorance regarding the nature of his divinity. The application of the divine spiritual wisdom is the only solution for those who are confronted with various psychological pressures and problems. This sacred wisdom is the golden key needed to open the door for people to experience superconsciousness in consciousness. It will help us heal and empower ourselves and help others do the same. It is necessary to have a system which allows us to see the unseen and know the unknown in order to gracefully face the challenges of time and space. *Lifting the Veil* gives you the basic layout of how the Universe works. It reveals the sacred blueprint by which we must live in this age in order to be healthy and experience the grace and divinity of universal intelligence. This system gives you early warnings of pitfalls, so that you may save yourself from unnecessary misfortune or adversity. *Lifting the Veil* reveals truths that will clear your mind, nurture your spirit and bring healing warmth to your heart. They are designed to make your journey through life happy, successful and fulfilling.

In this new age the proof of a spiritual practice must be measured by its successful application to everyday affairs. My hope is to present the divine spiritual wisdom in a way that everyone, even those who do not have any knowledge of Universal Kabbalah, may be able to understand it. Everyone can find a practical application of the system revealed in this book to the most ordinary aspects of everyday life. You will be so convinced of its truth that you may want to make it the guiding principle of all your daily actions.

For centuries Kabbalah and Kundalini yoga have been kept secret by the elite, who transmitted their practices selectively. These two ancient and powerful sciences are not only vital for spiritual growth but are also extremely helpful in understanding one's Self in relation to the Universe. This is the "age of no secrets," and these useful technologies can no longer remain hidden. Through the aid of these teachings, you can unite with your divinity and make the most of your potential and God-given gifts.

No one before has attempted to translate or interpret into language understood by the "people" the mystical symbolism of Kabbalah. They were busy mixing it into religion or associating it with the chosen few. As a result, the divine spiritual wisdom merely represents to many people one of the many doubtful superstitious practices which came to us from past ages. Whereas in fact, it is the mathematical application of proven laws. Kabbalah is the mathematics of spirituality. Facts have been painstakingly collected, experiments undertaken, and deductions made from collected data. Kabbalah and Kundalini yoga are systems of ancient wisdom that have been proven throughout the ages to have a healing and beneficial impact on our daily life when applied with sincerity and consistency.

Lifting the Veil reveals the underlying principle of the Universe and how it works. This book provides useful meditations that you can use on a daily basis to awaken your higher faculties, leading to improved health, more harmonious personal relationships, and an increased sense of peace and happiness. The practice of these principles will take away useless pain and unnecessary suffering from your life. *Lifting the Veil* will show you simple and practical ways of working with the Sun, the Moon, and the planets in order to restore and maintain health, be happy and live a holy life. These timeless teachings will nurture your spirit and illuminate your life.

The great Architect of the Universe has designed everything with breathtaking accuracy. Everything from the biggest planet to the smallest atom follows precise laws of nature. Observing the sunrise, the sunset, the stars at night, the four seasons, the waxing and waning Moon, one cannot deny that they reflect a particular design and order. God not only created the various worlds, planets and humans, but also the laws that govern them. These truths are the governing laws which maintain order and harmony in the various levels of the Universe. As every one can see, the seasons, the days, and the years refer to the orderly way in which nature unfolds before our eyes. We already are unconsciously relying on the unfailing order of nature that causes spring to come right after the winter. We take for granted that winter is winter, and we forget that the same laws that govern the seasons, govern our health, love life, and destiny as well. We should therefore conduct our lives in a regular and orderly manner following the laws of nature.

The tragedy is that humanity is more occupied today in building instruments for the destruction of life than in the problems of life itself or in examining those healing laws which create, control, and support life. If humankind is to enter into the higher spiritual realms of evolution, whereby the highest spiritual values of the soul can be brought into manifestation here on earth, then we must honor the laws of nature. The knowledge of these laws will free humanity from the spiritual chains that have been imposed upon their mind, body and spirit. It is a universally accepted assumption that law rules the Universe. These laws which govern this Universe work for good when you obey them. As human beings, we must learn to direct our free will to bring our lives into harmony with the laws that govern this Universe, so that we may find a real purpose in our life and living. By learning these laws and bringing our life into harmony with these laws, our life will be happy and peaceful.

Being in harmony with the Universe means living according to the laws of nature. When we follow these laws, we become agents of the divine Architect of the Universe, thus contributing to a positive evolution of humankind. If a person fails to act in accordance with the universal laws, then unhappiness, frustration, pain and disease set in. When you are out of harmony with the divine order of things, you attract disharmony and disunity. You will find yourself swimming against the tide, getting nowhere and simply exhausting yourself. Ceasing to be in harmony with these laws would in itself be to slip out of heaven and back into limitation.

By disobeying the laws of nature, we become our own worst enemies and bring suffering and punishment on ourselves while creating difficulties for others. Disobey them, and you will find yourself slipping downhill through sometimes many lives until you realize where you have gone astray and are determined to correct it. When you work against the laws you are fighting a losing battle and will get nowhere. Please keep in mind, the purpose of this book is not about restricting or infusing fear in you. Rather, *Lifting the Veil* will help you untie the knot of unawareness and ignorance, the worst disease of humankind. When you follow the law of the Universe, the Universe obeys you. There is no other way. This is why in this age of Light and truth, the Universe is raising our conscious-ness, so that we may recognize and align ourselves with the laws of nature that we have been violating for so long. Maintaining harmony with these laws will enhance our spiritual practice, bring light into our life and save us from past, present, and future darkness.

By constructively changing our behavior and attitude, and learning to honor God by our perfect obedience to his laws, we will undo and control the damages caused by the misuse of our free will, and our consciousness will grow and expand. Humans should study the order of the occurrences of happenings of nature, that which is called natural law. Above all, these teachings allow you to know yourself and when you find yourself you find God. By the study of the laws of nature, one comes close to God, for these are the laws of our creator. Without the knowledge of the unseen laws there can be no equilibrium in life, no balance on the scale of experience. After all, our experience of nature's laws and their manifestations as phenomena constitute a great scale that provides confidence and personal mastership in living. It is essential for us to obey the laws of nature in order to attach ourselves to the heavenly hierarchies, or luminous beings, so as to vibrate in unison with the whole Universe. Through yoga we get to know the structure of human; through Universal Kabbalah we relate to the immutable and universal laws as they are revealed to us.

Life can be compared to a battlefield where one must face both visible and invisible enemies. You can fight the visible ones, but the invisible enemies are difficult to conquer because it is almost impossible to fight what one cannot see. Not only do you need to know your enemies and the rules of combat, but you also need intuition. Your intuitive intelligence will give you 50 percent of the skill you need to fight. Understanding the rules will provide you with 40 percent. Therefore, all you need is 10 percent to win. Kundalini yoga will strengthen your intuition so you will be ready to tackle challenges.

Of the many spiritual paths and teachings available on Earth, I have found Kundalini yoga as taught by Yogi Bhajan—master of White Tantric and Kundalini yoga—to be one of the best sciences for developing intuition and elevating one's consciousness. My experience is that Yogi Bhajan is a supreme spiritual technician of our time. He was the first to make the bold move of publicizing the precious and priceless teachings of Kundalini yoga. When he first began to open this knowledge to all in 1969, most secret organizations were still selectively passing sacred teachings to a chosen few.

By making Kundalini yoga public, Yogi Bhajan has dramatically improved the lives of countless people.

The time we spend on the spiritual path should make us, if nothing else, very intuitive. The pituitary gland, our sixth chakra, is the master gland and the seat of the third eye. When that gland works, we are in tune with the Universe. We make the right decisions and react properly. However, if that gland is not working, our intuition cannot guide us, and we end up making terrible choices which can be very costly. Luckily, many of the Kundalini yoga meditations stimulate the pituitary gland, thereby activating intuition.

Let's face the truth. We can do a hundred things right, but one wrong move can destroy our whole life. We can have as much money as we want and still be in the wrong place at the wrong time. We can be very famous and find ourselves at the center of a scandal which will destroy our reputation and reduce our fame to notoriety. Everyday we see this in the news. We can have many degrees and find ourselves in a stressful job where we run the fearful risk of being fired. This long-term stress may lead to health complications. We can be physically beautiful and still contract a serious illness that no amount of money can help cure. Although I don't want to sound negative, these are the realities of life. It does not matter who we are, what we do, how beautiful we look, or how much money we have. What truly matters is our knowledge of the laws of nature, for it is the understanding of the forces of nature that will liberate us from the unhealthy habits that keep us in the cycle of negative patterns.

The realization that humans can be tossed around by unseen forces will call upon our awareness and move us from duality to divinity. Timing is everything. Knowledge of the best time to act or remain still is as vital as breathing. Taking the time to see which way the powerful forces of nature are moving, coupled with personal responsibility, will give us a repertoire of expanded options in our actions. A person who does not know what and when to do anything is at the mercy of whatever life throws his/her way.

Life does not have to be a guessing game. There are unfavorable and favorable periods for everyone. When times are unfavorable for you, save your energy—regroup and wait until the storm passes. Do not start anything new. By doing so, you will spare yourself from much unnecessary struggle. One can minimize adversity and misfortune by simply working with the timeless wisdom revealed in this book.

Before we start any project, it must have a probability of success. For this reason, it is our right and blessing to use some of the practical tools that the ancient students of nature have found most effective. After almost three decades of experience on this subject, I am so convinced of the truth of what is revealed in this book, that I only ask you to give the system a fair trial. I am certain that you will no longer ascribe the course of your life to "chance." To do so is to insult our creator. Genuine spiritual knowledge gives understanding, confidence and mastership. *Lifting the Veil* reveals a spiritual method whose efficacy has been tested and proven by time.

Part I

It does not matter who we are,
what we do, how beautiful we look,
or how much money we have.
What truly matters is our knowledge
of the laws of nature, for it is the
understanding of the forces of nature that
will liberate us from the unhealthy habits
that keep us in the cycle of negative patterns.

—Joseph Michael Levry (Gurunam)

Chapter One

Illuminating Truths

Before I proceed further, I need to say the following: The holy wisdom of Kabbalah should in no way be mixed with religion. Historically speaking, humankind should remember the connection between religion and the tragedy of the great Library of Alexandria in old Egypt. All the healing and spiritual knowledge known to the world was preserved in the library of Alexandria for future genera-tions. As a result of religion these transcripts were set on fire in the baths and bake houses of Alexandria. The loss of these spiritual teachings has been described as the single most tragic loss and the greatest disaster ever recorded. If this library existed today, there isn't enough money in this world that could buy this healing bank of teachings.

Religions are aspects of universal truths revealed at a given time, to a given people, in given circumstances. Unfortunately, over time the teachings can become twisted by self-serving parties who rein-terpret them as being the sole and only revealed truth, valid for all men, at all times, in all circumstances. This is how intolerance, conflict, war and persecutions are perpetrated, which is contrary to the original divine revelations. Whether we like it or not, we are all interconnected. Not being able to see God in everyone causes fear, separation and hatred. Not being able to see God in oneself leads to the inability to forgive oneself and others. This further gener-ates anger that destroys so many lives. Those who cannot see God in every sacred teaching, in everyone, and in themselves cannot see God at all. By this, they become the channel of dark forces and cause unthinkable evil acts that disrupt humanity. Therefore, religion, although pure in its original intention, seeks to control and divide. History has shown us, through numerous examples, what religion has done. The true meaning of religion practiced in churches, mosques, synagogues, and temples is to know God, who exists equally and impartially in every human being. Kabbalah and yoga enable one to perceive the truth in all sacred teachings. Do not give your power away. Claim it, and use it for good.

My intention is not to turn you into an intellectual Kabbalist. In my various travels, I have encountered many intellectual Kabbalists who could dazzle your mind with beautiful Kabbalistic concepts, but who were completely lost when it came to practical application of those concepts in daily life. You can read a number of books and become more confused than when you started, because ninety percent of the writings on the subject are not only complex but very misleading. There are also teachers who claim to possess the pure science, yet preach divisive ideas and pass the information only to a select group of people. They forget that every human being is a ray of the Sun. Those teachers do not possess the divine fire. They always start with many students, but the number sooner or later drops because their essence is not pure. Teachers and books simply remind you of what is already within you.

On the other hand, there are people who collect various initiations from teachers and spiritual organizations, hoping to be illuminated. It is important for you to know that no human being can initiate you. Only the Universe, to whom you are completely transparent, can do it. When you are ready, the invisible world lifts the veil of ignorance and activates the divine fire in you, creating the condition for true illumination. Only then do you start to see God in everyone, including yourself. Also, you see God in every teaching and can merge them all. Those who have the divine fire are so radiant that they shine like the Sun. It is extremely uplifting to be in their company. Their intention is to unite all people. The way they communicate is so special that anyone, regardless of their level, can understand them.

Everyone must understand the necessity to seek to live in closer harmony with God and his nature and thus in peace with oneself and one's neighbor. As Universal Kabbalists, we are and must be leaders. We must set the example in developing ourselves in a constructive and genuine spiritual way. To develop ourself is to raise our vibrations. To raise our vibrations is to positively influence everyone who comes into contact with us. We need to rise beyond isolation, bigotry, prejudice and narrow-mindedness. By our living example, we can help change darkness into light. For each person who develops himself, lifts the human race along with him to that extent. For us to be secure, we must change our attitude and become universal in order to help raise the individual and collective consciousness.

God did not make Christian, Jews, Hindus, Muslims or Buddhists—these are distinctions that we created. Each one of us is a ray of the beautiful Sun. The Sun, a visible symbol of the light of our creator, shines on every one alike. God also did not separate humans into nationalities and races. That is the effect of climate and evolution, conditions that have come upon humanity since it was created. It is humans who used these differences to divide us. We must remember that humankind needs to unite so we can work towards our own reintegration. It is time for us to be bold, to lead humankind to this beautiful transformation through our thoughts, words, and deeds.

Also, it seems reasonable to suppose that the apparent complexity and myths associated with the Kabbalah is largely due to the lack of cooperation on the part of certain Kabbalists to recognize that while the truths, laws, and principles, contained in the Kabbalah are eternal, they must be restated and put in terms commensurate with the growth of knowledge. No one needs to fear to do just that, for truth is truth. Everything is evolving. The same is true for the human brain, nothing ever is, but is ever becoming. The brain of a twenty-first century Kabbalist has evolved from the fourteenth-century brain. Our realities are not the same. Growth is inevitable and necessary. Even if it is a fact that every forward step ever made or likely to be made has always been and will continue to be contested. It is also true, that sooner or later the contestants become the followers of the daring few, thus forcing them to take another step onward. The duty of the divine spiritual wisdom is to enable a human to harmoniously cope with the forces of nature.

The fact is, no human is truly educated until one has learned the divine spiritual wisdom. As yogi, Kabbalist or human we must make the time to study the sacred teachings, and then use those teachings to be of service to humankind. Furthermore, not only must we have some understanding of God as a supreme being, we must understand that every one of our fellow humans is part of that absolute being, and therefore we must treat them as such.

Chapter Two

Kabbalah

A word of warning: if you are learning any spiritual teaching and you start to develop a superiority complex that makes you think that you belong to an elect group or the chosen few, you seriously need to reexamine yourself. Whether we like it or not, we are all interconnected. We must realize that the human race is one and we all share a common divine ancestry. The whole world is to each of us our own family. It is by working together that we can all make it. No one will be saved until we all are. My sincere wish is for you to become a practical Kabbalist, but I also think that it is important to have some background information on the subject.

There are two major books of Kabbalah. The first is the *Sepher Yetzirah*, or *Book of Formation*, which tradition traces back to Abraham. The second book is the *Zohar*, or *Book of Splendor*, which was written during the thirteenth century in Aramaic in Spain, by a Kabbalist named Moses de Leon. The holy wisdom came from the land of Mizraim of ancient Egypt, which spread to Chaldea, Persia, India, China, Japan, Greece, Rome, etc. The Egyptians, the Babylonians and the Chaldeans were particularly well versed in the Kabbalah. According to history, the Hebrew people learned it when they were held captive in Egypt and later mixed it with Judaism.

Among the people in ancient Egypt with pristine power was Hermes Trismegistus, the Master of Masters. It is believed that he lived to be about 145 years old, and that Abraham learned some of the knowledge of the Kabbalah from this thrice-great master. Those who followed Hermes always passed this holy wisdom to a select few. This is where the principle of secrecy originated. This explains why the knowledge of Kabbalah has traditionally been disseminated to only a limited number of initiates. It is for these reasons that Kabbalah is so unknown to most people.

Kabbalah, which was regarded for many centuries as the key to the Universe, is one of the oldest systems of mystical thought in the world. It not only explains the relation between the microcosm (Man) and the macrocosm (Universe), but it also reveals the means of uniting with the Godhead. Kabbalah is rooted in the traditional arcana. The word Kabbalah, which means *receiving*, refers to the revelation that God made to humans by the medium of Metatron, who is the Archangel closest to God.

It is very important to know that almost every philosopher and religious thinker, from the founder of the Essenes to Roger Bacon, has had an influence on the Kabbalah. Even Helen Petrona Blavatsky chose the name "The Secret Doctrine," which is known by most middle-age thinkers, to name her compilation of esoteric occultism. There is a frequently ignored Judeo-Christian trend to Kabbalah. On one hand, there is Judaic Kabbalah which can be presented on two levels. The first level is made up of the basic principles of Kabbalah. It is called the *Ta Amei Torah*. The second level is made up of the "secrets" of Kabbalah, which is called the *Si Trei Torah*. On the other hand there are the Rose+Croix Kabbalists, and their work can be summarized in the following manner: healing the sick and giving anonymous help to individuals, organizations or states, if their cause is just. It is also said that they engage in political action leading to the establishment of a vast universal state to re-integrate man and nature into their original estate. This program was eventually given to less mysterious organizations, which were closer to the profane world.

Among those initiatic movements, the most well known are Martinism and Freemasonry. The forefathers of America, for example, were Freemasons. It is those mystical philosophers and Freemasons who laid the foundation for national unity and helped direct the course of the revolution. The seven signers of the United States Declaration of Independence are known to have been Freemasons. For example, Benjamin Franklin was a past Master of the Pennsylvania

Freemasons when he helped draft the declaration of independence. Thomas Jefferson was a Freemason. He served as the Master of the lodge of the nine Muses while he was in France. George Washington was also a Freemason. This is shown by the Masonic collar, sash, and apron that he wore, while laying the cornerstone of the capitol. It is the Freemasons who laid the foundation for national unity in America, and this eventually gave birth to the United States. They were, and still are, the moving force in all key areas of America and many other western countries.

The great seal of the United States, designed by Freemasons and reproduced on the dollar bill, symbolized a lineage into the tradition of the ancient mysteries. The Latin words *Novus Ordo Seclorum* or the New Order of the Ages, represents the Great Work done by the Freemasons. They sealed their work with the following Latin words *Annuit Coeptis* or "God has smiled on our undertakings." The United States seal is based upon the Masonic virtues symbolized by the colors in the American flag: red represents fortitude, pure white relates to temperance, and blue stands for justice and prudence. Freemasonry is about achieving the Great Work by raising man's consciousness and spiritual faculties, so that he may become a perfect instrument for the Great Architect of the Universe to use for manifesting the glory of heaven on Earth. The two branches of Martinism and Freemasonry collaborate together to realize this program of the Rosicrucians in the social and political spheres.

Martinism was given a task, which is more occult and esoteric. For the realization of their vast plan, covering several necessary centuries of modern times, the Rose+Croix used the whole traditional occult knowledge: the vast complex of astrological, alchemical and occult symbology, the teachings of the Rose+Croix, the Masonic Myths, and the tarot, which include spargyrie, magic, theurgy, divination, and the use of supernatural means for the great work. Their doctrine is a combination of Christian Gnosis and Judaic Kabbalah. They are, in fact, Christian Kabbalists. The basis of Kabbalah is essentially a Gnostic symbol, known as the Tree of Life, which consist of ten circles joined by twenty-two lines. It symbolizes the creation as a fall from the ultimate Godhead to the kingdom of earth. In other words, our soul begins its journey downwards, progressing through ten spheres and ending in a state of amnesia in the human or earthly body.

According to Kabbalah, humankind is like a group of cells. Each person is a cell or unit in the body of Adamic Humanity, and the privation and relative darkness in which we dwell is a result of Human's symbolic fall from an original state of glory and oneness with the Divine Being, for Man-God, known in Kabbalah as *Adam Kadmon*, was originally a unified being. Before the fall, this collective man had a glorious spiritual form and was living on a higher spiritual plane enjoying the most incredible privileges. After the misuse of free will, Adam or Man-God, was cast out of that higher plane and lost his pristine position and spiritual privileges. As a result of the fall, this unified being became fragmented, and the cells of that being are now the souls of the men and women we now refer to as humanity. As you can naturally deduce from the above, every man and woman is connected. We are each one cell of Adam Kadmon.

The divine spiritual wisdom reveals how the soul can achieve reunion with the Godhead. The soul can realize the union, only through detaching itself from the earthly body, and making its way back through the nine spheres. Kabbalah is the foundation stone of the Western esoteric mystery tradition, just as the Yoga Sutras, the Upanishads, the Bhagavad Gita, the Stanzas of Dyzan, and other holy works are the foundations of Eastern traditions. Kabbalah, in its entirety, is the great body of philosophy, which is associated with the Judaic mystic tradition, but was originally practiced by the ancient Egyptians.

Kabbalah is found in the Old Testament of the Bible, particularly the Pentateuch, and the vast complex of astrological, alchemical and occult symbology, the teachings of the Rose+ Croix, the Masonic Myths, and the tarot. Originally, the Kabbalah was considered to be so holy that it was reserved entirely as an oral tradition, that is, it was handed down since biblical times strictly "from mouth to ear."

As mentioned earlier, you will find the teachings of Kabbalah in the Bhagavad Gita, the Yoga Sutras, the Stanzas and many more holy books. It is so vast a subject that it is difficult to find a person who can master it all. Because of the persecution of the Christian church and its desire to control, the holy wisdom had to be hidden and preserved in a simple and mighty symbol called the Tree of Life (see page 25 for illustration). The key to all the mysteries of the Universe is contained in it. It is a huge library, in which all the secrets of humankind and the Universe are revealed. The Tree of Life shows how we come to this world of suffering, disease and pain. Not only does it show how to return to our origin, but it also reveals how humanity can live happily while on Earth. As a matter of fact, the basis of the holy Kabbalah is the sacred Tree of Life, which consists of ten spheres linked together by the 22 paths, which are related to the 22 major arcana of the tarot cards. Kabbalah used to be a system where devoted students would meditate on the ten aspects of God revealed by each of those spheres. These ten spheres, known as Sephiroth or the emanations of life, are basically a Gnostic diagram. They correspond to different levels of our mental, spiritual and physical life. Again, as mentioned above, each of the ten spheres on the Tree of Life also corresponds to one of the planetary bodies. In order, we have Neptune, Uranus, Saturn, Jupiter, Mars, Sun, Venus, Mercury, Moon and Earth. Each of these spheres/planets has an Archangel who in turn is in charge of the angels of that particular area. They are respectively governed by the Archangels Metatron, Raziel, Tsaphkiel, Tsadkiel, Kamael, Raphael, Hanael, Michael, Gabriel and Sandalfon. The top circle, Kether, is the unknown, the unseen, which is often referred to as ether, whereas the bottom circle, Malkuth, represents the known, the seen, which symbolizes the Earth.

In other words, the Universe is divided into ten regions or Sephiroth corresponding to the ten spheres of the Tree of Life. (The word sephiroth, the plural of sephirah, means numeration). Each Sephirah is identified by five names: The name of God, the name of the Sephirah itself, the name of the angelic order and finally the name of one of the planets. Each Sephirah is a region inhabited by an order of luminous beings under the leadership of an Archangel who is subject to the almighty God. It is God who governs the ten regions under a different name in each.

Each Sephirah of the Tree of Life expresses a particular aspect of the Divine Harmony. God has ten names which correspond to ten different attributes; it is the same God seen under ten different aspects. Each of these ten aspects are equal.

The ten names of God are:
Eheieh
Yah
Jehovah (Elohim)
El
Elohim Gibor
Jehovah Eloah Va-Daath
Jehovah Tzevaot *or* **Adonoy Tzevaos**
Elohim Tzevaot
Shaddai El Chai
Adonoy Ha Aretz

The names of the ten Sephiroth are:
Kether: Crown
Chokmah: Wisdom
Binah: Understanding
Chesed: Mercy
Geburah: Strength
Tiphareth: Beauty
Netzach: Victory
Hod: Glory
Yesod: Foundation
Malkuth: Kingdom

The leaders of the Angelic Orders are:
   Metatron: He who stands by the throne
   Raziel: Secret of God
   Tzaphkiel: Contemplation of God
   Tzadkiel: Justice of God
   Kamael: Desire of God
   Raphael: Healing of God
   Haniel: Grace of God
   Mikhael: Who is like God
   Gabriel: Power of God
   Uriel: God is my light, or
   Sandalfon: Who is seen as the force that binds matter to form

The Angelic Orders are:
   Hayoth Hakadesh: Holy living creatures, or seraphim
   Ophanim: Wheels or cherubim
   Aralim: Thrones the mighty ones
   Chashmalim: Shining ones or dominations
   Seraphim: Fiery ones, or powers
   Malachim: King of splendor or Archangels
   Elohim: Gods or principalities
   Benei Elohim: Sons of god or virtues
   Kerubim: Strong ones or angels
   Ishim: Men, or the communion of saints

Last we have the ten planets corresponding to our physical body:

Rashith Ha Galgalim	First Swirlings
Mazaloth	The Zodiac
Shabbathai	Saturn
Tsedek	Jupiter
Maadim	Mars
Shemesh	Sun
Noga	Venus
Kokab	Mercury
Levanah	Moon
Aretz	Earth

In reality, Kabbalah is very simple, since it reveals much profound knowledge in the form of symbols. Images and symbols are the language used by humanity to communicate with the astral world. The power of the truth remains in its simplicity; anything that is complicated is not the truth. If it's the truth, it should be simple. If it is not simple, it is not truth. Surrounding it with secrecy, under the pretext of preventing its misuse, is nonsense. The learning of Kabbalah creates a positive metamorphosis in anyone who studies it. Truth is light, and darkness cannot stand in the presence of light. Learning Kabbalah is like absorbing light that automatically dispels the darkness of misuse. Since we are now in the Age of Light, and knowledge can no longer be kept hidden, it is time for humanity to become familiar with what the Kabbalah has to reveal.

A Kabbalist is a spiritual person who, by honest and serious divine work, has elevated himself to the level of a pure servant of the Universe. He or she is filled with so much love and compassion that he sees God in everyone. He sees God in every sacred teaching, and he sees God in himself. He or she is ageless, raceless, classless and genderless. Bear in mind that those who cannot see God in everyone, cannot see God at all. Those who cannot see God in any sacred teaching, cannot see God at all. Those who cannot see God in themselves, cannot see God at all. They are neither a true Kabbalist, nor a real yogi. It would be deceitful to claim to love God in one person and fail to see Him in another. The same is true for any sacred teaching and yourself.

Intuition and the Holy Kabbalah

After almost three decades of extensive work with universal Kabbalah and Kundalini yoga guiding individuals to heal and rise from crossroads, I can honestly say that it is neither enough to practice yoga alone nor is it sufficient to work only with Kabbalah, for in regard to intuition, most untrained people are only twenty percent intuitive. It is a fact that the practice of meditation and yoga, can have your intuition work at the level of sixty percent.

Although yoga will help balance your mind, body, and spirit, you still need to know how the Universe works, otherwise you will lack the true essence of timing and be faced with limitations. Those laws give you light. It is that light which shows you the way, by giving you optimal intuition. Without light you will meet with every obstacle, and your time and energy will be eaten by frustration, anxiety, fear, and anger.

God gave free will to all of us to use in making decisions every day. Every minute of life is a challenge full of choices. Poor choices cause us suffering; good choices bring us happiness. We can avoid a lot of pain through the use of our intuition. Most of us hardly use our intuition, because we have not been trained to listen and hone our inner ear. Intuition is the guidance of the soul. It is the soul talking to us, guiding us through the jungle of life. A person without intuition or inner hearing has neither direction nor command. He or she is often tossed around by fate, and sooner or later suffers the consequences of foolish acts.

The practice of Universal Kabbalah will enable you to wisely and harmoniously merge with this universal flow so that you may intuitively and gracefully face the challenges of time and space. Actually, Kabbalists need yoga and yogis can use Universal Kabbalah in the same way the east and west complement each other. For the Eastern world is as spiritual or intuitive as the right brain hemisphere, and the Western world is as logical as the left brain hemisphere. Therefore, the unique mixture of the sacred teachings of Kabbalah and Kundalini yoga is being called upon. Universal Kabbalah is harmoniously blending and weaving together the energy of Kabbalah and Kundalini yoga while casting off the illusionary aspects of the Kabbalah. Universal Kabbalah holds fast only to the element of divinity that shines within both systems of truth and understanding. This is symbolized by the neutral brain, which is activated as a result of the balance of both brain hemispheres thereby causing the divine glands—pituitary and pineal glands—to bestow intuitive logic upon us so that we may gracefully move through life.

This offers an incredibly powerful spiritual platform for those who are on the path of light and just beginning the work that will continue to help them blossom. The divine spiritual wisdom teaches us how the Universe (macrocosm) and humankind (microcosm) were created. It also reveals how one can change space and affect destiny through understanding the seven planets. It impacts intuitive logic through the merging of logic and intuition. Intuitive logic is the highest form of both intuition and logic. It is direct knowing. This logic has one duty, and that is to justify intuition.

This wisdom can make one universally intuitive. Such knowledge can eliminate all decisions based on trial and error. Guesswork will always bring pain, and life should not be a gamble. Nothing was ever done by chance. The Universe was mathematically built, and there is a natural rhythm to nature—a flow to the Universe.

THE TREE OF LIFE

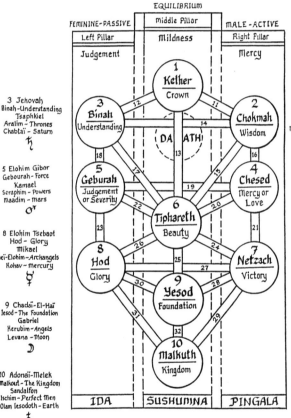

1 Ehieh
Kether - The Crown
Metatron
Hayot Ha-Kodesch - Seraphs
Reschit Ha-Galgalim - The first vortex (Neptune)

EQUILIBRIUM

FEMININE-PASSIVE   Middle Pillar   MALE-ACTIVE

Left Pillar   Mildness   Right Pillar

Judgement   Mercy

1
Kether
Crown

3 Jehovah
Binah-Understanding
Tsaphkiel
Aralim – Thrones
Chabtaï – Saturn

3
Binah
Understanding

12   11

14

DAATH
13

2
Chokmah
Wisdom

2 Iah
Hokmah – Wisdom
Raziel
Ophanim – Cherubim
Mazaloth – The Zodiac (Uranus)

5 Elohim Gibor
Gebourah - Force
Kamael
Seraphim – Powers
Maadim – Mars

18   17   16

5
Geburah
Judgement
or Severity

19

22   20

4
Chesed
Mercy or
Love

4 El
Hesed – Mercy
Tsadkiel
Hachmalim – Dominations
Tsedek – Jupiter

6
Tiphareth
Beauty

8 Elohim Tsebaot
Hod – Glory
Mikael
Bneï-Elohim – Archangels
Kohav – Mercury

23   21

26   24

8
Hod
Glory

25

27

7
Netzach
Victory

7 Jehovah Tsebaot
Netzach – Victory
Haniel
Elohim – Principalities
Noga – Venus

9 Chadaï-El-Haï
Iesod - The Foundation
Gabriel
Kerubim – Angels
Levana – Moon

30   28

9
Yesod
Foundation

31   29

32

6 Eloha ve Daath
Tipheret - Beauty
Raphaël
Malahim – Virtues
Chemesch – Sun

10 Adonaï-Melek
Malkout - The Kingdom
Sandalfon
Ischim – Perfect Men
Olam Iesodoth - Earth

10
Malkuth
Kingdom

IDA   SUSHUMNA   PINGALA

There is no chance, no destiny, no fate
that can circumvent or hinder
or control the firm resolve of a determined soul.
Gifts count for nothing; will alone is great;
all things give way before it, sooner or later.
What obstacle can stay the mighty force
of the sea-seeking river in its course,
or cause the ascending orb of day to wait?
Each well-born soul must win what it deserves;
let the fool prate of luck.
The fortunate is he whose earnest purpose never swerves,
whose slightest action or inaction
serves the one great aim.
Why even death stands still,
and waits an hour sometimes
for such a will.

—by Ella Wheeler Wilcox, from "Will"

Chapter Three

Kundalini Yoga

What Kabbalah is to the West, Kundalini yoga is to the East. Kundalini yoga is the science of awareness. It is known as the mother of all yogas and the yoga of royalty. It is the uncoiling and utilization of energy that lies latent within us all. Kundalini yoga creates an integration of the mind, body, and spirit. The exercises and meditations in Kundalini yoga help purify, stimulate, and strengthen all the systems of the body, particularly the digestive, nervous, and glandular systems. Kundalini Yoga strengthens the nerves, removes toxins, charges the electro-magnetic field, alters one's state of mind, and purifies the blood.

Kundalini yoga is the science of becoming nothing, so that everything can come to you. It is the science of awareness and Christic consciousness. It shows the way to illumination. In the words of Yogi Bhajan, master of Kundalini yoga:

"I have recognized, with the blessing of my Master, that it is possible to be healthy, to be happy, and to be holy while living in this society; but you must have energy so that your dead computer may live and pass on the signal to you and may compute all that you want to do in this society. We call this energy, in the olden science, the Kundalini, which has been blocked in Muladhara, the lowest of all chakras or lotuses. There is a way we should set our computer to be in direct contact with Him, the Biggest Computer, and all things must then work automatically. That cannot work until the Kundalini, the spiritual nerve, breaks through the blockage at the Muladhara, and thus travels up and reaches the stage so that you may have superconsciousness in consciousness.

"You must generate the pressure of the prana and mix it with the apana, and thus, when the two join together, you generate heat in the pranic center. With this heat of the prana, you put a pressure or charge on the Kundalini, the soul nerve, which is coiled in three and a half circles (*kundal* means the curl of the hair of the beloved; it does not mean snake or serpent) on Muladhara. This will awaken it so that it may pierce through the imaginary chakras and pass ultimately through Jalandhara Bandha (neck lock—the final blockage in the spine before the energy reaches the head).

"Now let me define a few terms. Prana is the life-force of the atom. Apana is elimination, or the eliminating force. These are two forces, positive and negative, in us which are governed by *pingala* and *ida*; that is, right and left. (In the Tree of Life there is the pillar of Mercy, the pillar of Judgment, and the pillar of Equilibrium. Ida stands for the pillar of Judgment and pingala the pillar of Mercy.) When we join these two energies under the power and the science of Kundalini Yoga, we mix the prana with the apana and, under that pressure, bring the Kundalini up. When it passes through the central nerve of Sushamana, it reaches the higher chakras or lotuses, and thus man can easily look into the future. His psychic power becomes activated. He can know his total surroundings and he is a blessed being.

"After one inhales the prana deep (down to the navel point) and pulls the apana with the root lock (up to the navel point), prana and apana mix at the navel center. This is known as Nibhi Chakra at the fourth vertebra. Heat is felt during the Kundalini awakening and that heat is the filament of the Sushamana, or central spinal channel, being lit by the joining of prana and apana. Below the Nibhi

Chakra, the energy leaves the navel and goes to the rectum (or lower center) and then it rises. This is called Reserve Channels. It relates to your Astral Body. Then, there are six more chakras through which the Kundalini must rise—and it will happen all at once. Once you have raised it, that's it. The hardest job is to keep it up to keep the channels clean and clear.

"From the rectum to the vocal cord is known as the silver cord. From the neck to the top of the head is the passage. From the third eye to the pineal gland is the gold cord. To make the energy rise in these cords and passages, you must apply hydraulic locks. You must put a pressure. You live in California? You know how we take the oil out of the ground? Put a pressure and the oil will come out. Your spine is a stair-case of energy. 1) Mulabandha brings apana, eliminating force, to the navel or fourth vertebra, the central seat of the Kundalini. 2) Diaphragm lock takes it to the neck. 3) Neck lock takes it up all the rest of the way.

"The pineal gland, or seat of the soul, does not work when the tenth gate (top of the head) is sealed, but if the pineal will secrete (when the Kundalini heat comes), your pituitary will act as radar, keeping the mind from negativity. Yes, Kundalini is known as the nerve of the soul. This is to be awakened. Your soul is to be awakened. When soul gets awakened, there remains nothing. What else?

"In the practical reality, these chakras are imaginary and nothing else. This Kundalini is just a Kundalini and nothing else. It is not very important. These pranas and apanas are just there. Everything is set in us. We lack nothing. We use these terms simply to make the process clear so we can get on with it. It is very simple. After getting myself into the darkness for years together, I found that if I would have known on the first day that it was so easy, I could have saved myself a lot of hassle. When I found out that the Kundalini really can come up like this, I was astonished. It was a surprise to me. I said, 'That's all there is to Kundalini?' and my Master said, 'Yes.'

"All it is, is creating the prana in the cavity and mixing it with apana and taking it down (as we give pressure to the oil) and bringing the oil up. This is Kundalini. That's it. That is the greatest truth. Truth is bitter I know, so I cannot speak all the truth; but I speak indirectly and directly about the truth because I cannot speak something beyond truth."

—*From lectures by and conversations with Yogi Bhajan, 1969*

Cosmic Consciousness

The true and ultimate purpose of all spiritual or religious practice is to awaken this mighty and evolutionary force called Kundalini— the mother of eternal happiness.

The miraculous answer to prayers, the expression of human genius in any field of endeavor, performing miracles or demonstrating spiritual power, including instant healing, are linked to a voluntary or accidental release of a tiny amount of this infinite force in the *shusmuna*.

The awakening of this evolutionary force generates an expansion in consciousness which spiritualizes, illuminates and regenerates a human being turning him or her into a genius. Throughout history humans of all ages who have experienced the release of a particular amount of this force have given birth to wonderful and breathtaking works of art and music in philosophy, religion, poetry and theatre.

The activity of this force raises one's consciousness leading to illumination. In fact, true illumination or cosmic consciousness has been known to manifest through one organ; it is located in the heart. It turns the heart into spiritual gold causing the soul to express its genius.

It is cosmic consciousness that caused Leonardo Da Vinci to give birth to the magnificent painting *Mona Lisa*, presently located in the Louvre museum of Paris, France. Among those who have been illuminated and whose work have touched humankind, we have the great philosophers of Greece such as Plato and Aristotle. We also have great names such as Pythagoras, Lao Tse, Zoroaster, Confucius, Gautama the Buddha, Mohammed, Moses, etc. Their work became immortal like the following alchemists, as well as Rose+Croix Kabbalists:

Hermes Trismegistus, the Egyptian sage (1399–1257 B.C.)
"Hermes the Thrice-great," "Lord of the Maat," "Lord of Books." So-called founder and father of Alchemy. His veiled writings are so outstanding that the uninitiated consider Hermes a myth, or confuse him with Thoth the Egyptian God. To this day, his Emerald Tablet of mystical precepts has been most highly valued by mystics. Over 30,000 contributions to the Art attributed to him. He died at the Rosicrucian Monastery at El Amarna at age 142.

Maria the Jewess
Recognized as the first woman alchemist. Occasionally thought to be Miriam, sister of Moses. Credited with the invention of various chemical apparatus, and with the perfection of distillation. She knew the hidden secrets of the great stone.

Democritus the Grecian (460–362 B.C.)
Known as the "laughing philosopher," Democritus was a Rose+ Croix Master who cosmically received the atomic conception of the Universe. He wrote seventy-two works on physics, mathematics, ethics, and grammar. Einstein called him a "religious genius," great because he was guided by "a cosmic religious sense." Certain alchemical writings attributed to Democritus are actually by Bolos of Mende, a Hellenized Egyptian living around 200 B.C.

Morienus the Roman Alexandrian
An Orthodox Christian hermit. Pious mystic. Allegedly transmuted base metals into gold before Arabian Prince Khalid. "God commands his carefully chosen servants that they seek out this divine and

pious - having or showing a dutiful spirit or reverance
for God or an earnest regard for religious
obligations.

holy science… This knowledge takes its possessor away from the suffering of this world and leads him to the knowledge of future blessing…"

Avicenna the Arabian (Abu Ali ibn Sina; 980–1037 A.D.)
Known as the Aristotle of the Arabians, the Leading Wise Man in the East and Prince of the Physicians in the West, the Muslim mystic of Bokhara, Persia, was an authority on medicine at 16. Soon after, mastered Islamic law and metaphysics. Heavily influenced theory and practice of medicine in the Middle Ages. He created new compounds and distilled medicines with his vast knowledge of alchemy. His writings on medicine and the sciences brought him great renown in both East and West. Developed a mystical theosophy as well.

Albertus Magnus the German (Albert von Bollstedt, Albert de Groot, Doctor Universalis—"the universal Doctor"; 1193–1282)
Prominent scholastic philosopher of the 13th century. Dominican Bishop. Called "magnus" for greatness in learning and wisdom in many fields. Great writer, valued as collector of alchemical data rather than innovator. His writings popularized theories and facts of chemistry among educated classes. Maier said Alberus received from the disciples of St. Dominic the Philosopher's Stone, which in turn was communicated by him to St. Thomas Aquinas, his student.

Roger Bacon the Englishman (Doctor Mirabilis—"the wonderful Doctor"; 1214–1292)
Great Franciscan theologian, thinker, philosopher. Studied optics and mathematics at Oxford. Dominating position in 13th century science; first exponent of the deductive method. Zealous, inventive student, magnetic healer, practical alchemist, divided alchemy into two parts; experimental medicines, elixir, purification of metals, and comparative—the germ of chemical science. Bacon was known to have predicted and described automobiles, airplanes, high-speed sea travel, microscopes, telescopes, gunpowder, and test-tube babies. Known for his brilliant innovations.

Arnoldus Villanovus the Frenchman (Arnald of Villanova of Catalonia; 1240–1312)
Spanish physician of high repute, master of medicine at Barcelona and Paris. Great interest in magic and alchemy. Called alchemy "The Rosary of the Philosophers." Transmuted plates of copper into gold before minions of Pope Clement V. Visionary, mystical approach to alchemy, felt worker as well as materials must be unified and purified. Known for *Thesaurus Thesaurorum et Rosarium Philosphorum* (Treasure of Treasures and Rose Garden of the Philosophers.)

Thomas Aquinas the Italian (Saint Thomas Aquinas; 1225–1274)
Theologian, Father and Doctor of the Church. Arranged all knowledge in hierarchical order. Embraced sciences as explaining the physical aspects of existence, but to the Church he left the realm of God. The realm of revelation was said to transcend mortal reason. Religion, then, without remorse could condone chemistry, physics geometry, astronomy. Strongly believed that given the proper knowledge, the structure of matter could be refined and changed.

Raymond Lully the Spaniard (Raymundus Lullus; 1225–1315)
Lully's alleged last testament states that while in London he transmuted twenty-two tons of base metal into gold to enable King Edward II (or III) to fight the Turks. Credited by some with several thousand alchemical treatises. He wrote *Anima artis transmutationis* or *Clavicula*. He was held in high estimation of later alchemists. Minorite friar, prolific writer on theology, philosophy, logic, and so on.

Melchior Cibiensis the Hungarian
Of Szeben, Transylvania; "although a priest, he won golden gifts. Under the form of the Mass he described the Stone…" Maier described him as a Christian priest who had graduated in "the hidden mysteries of the hidden science." He wrote poetic descriptions of transmutation. The essential unity of the worlds of spirit and nature were revealed to him.

Sir Francis Bacon (1561–1625)
Lord Chancellor of England, scientist, philosopher, author, statesman. Editor of the King James version of the Bible and the first English essayist. He was a driving force in the Elizabethan Renaissance. He is thought by many to be the true but concealed author of the works of Shakespeare and other Elizabethan literature. In his well-known work *Novum Organum* Bacon presented a method of inductive logic. In *Instauratio Magna* he offered a plan for a complete reconstruction of sciences, arts, and all human knowledge to restore humanity to mastery over nature.

Anonymus Sarmata (Michael Sendivogius the Pole; 1562–1646)
Reportedly a gentleman of Cracow, Poland. Was bequeathed a quantity of the Powder of Projection by Alexander Seton, a Scottish alchemist Sendivogius saved from prison. Sendivogius married Seton's widow, and with the Powder made a name for himself. After many transmutations for royalty, served as a counselor of State to four emperors.

Rene Descartes (1596–1650)
French philosopher known for his famous *Gogito Ergo Sum*—I think therefore I am. He started modern philosophy.

Benjamin Franklin (1706–1790)
Most well-known for his work on electricity.

Don Martinez Pasqualles de la Tour (1710–1778)
Don Martinez de Pasqualles was a Rose+Croix Kabbalist of a peculiar kind who conjures up the picture of a man of mystery. He was the founder of the Masonic Rosicrucian group called the Elect Cohens. He established in Paris an order of so called "Illumine." He was born in Grenoble in 1710 and died in Haiti in 1778. He used to leave town without telling anybody where he was going, and he arrived at a place without revealing from where he had come. About such "high truths," as Louis Claude de St. Martin described

Martinez' teachings, he said, "I am persuaded that we would have arrived at them at last, had we kept him longer."

Louis Claude De Saint Martin (1743–1803)
He was initiated in the Elect Cohens in the second half of 1768. The effect was as deep as Cagliostro's induction in the Freemasons. Three years later, he left the army and devoted the remainder of his life to mysticism. From 1768 to 1771 served as personal secretary to Pasquales during which the character and teachings of the later made a profound impression on him. He published his first philosophical work *Of Errors and of Truth* when he was 32. This has been regarded by many as his most searching work and most fruitful contribution to the literature of esotericism. He was published under the pseudonym of "The Unknown Philosopher." Like Pythagoras, Saint Martin travelled to study man and nature and to compare the testimony of others to his own work. He lived on very little, accepting none of the profit. He delighted in going to the theatre, but many times on his way there he would turn back if he thought of someone in need to whom he would give the fare instead. By the time he died, Martinism was a European movement like Sweden borgianism. Of the orders of Illuminist Masonry which flowered in France during the 18th century, none has had an influence comparable to that which entered into history under the name of Martinism.

Count St. Germain
The wonderman of Europe; a leading figure in the Rosicrucians, Freemasons and Knights Templar. He was a gifted musician, artist, historian, alchemist, and linguist who spoke at least 12 languages.

As the few examples above show, when illumination comes, one's work becomes a masterpiece that moves every soul that comes in touch with it. Not only does it live forever, but it especially gives one appeal to every human heart.

Cosmic consciousness enables one to display a genuinely excellent personality that practices kindness and goodness and has respect for the common good. Such a soul understands, expresses, heals and uplifts every human being. It causes one to rise beyond selfish or personal needs, interests and experiences, thereby leading one to become interested in the advancement of the human race. As a result, one develops a healing personality which leaves a constructive and permanent influence upon the page of history or in the memory of humankind.

Cosmic consciousness or illumination enable one to see God in every teaching, in oneself, and in every human being. It allows one to develop and maintain an integrated personality which embodies values acceptable to society and individuals, but also reveals spiritual ideals of conduct which manifest the cumulative experience of wisdom of the human race.

To achieve illumination, work faithfully with the divine spiritual wisdom herein revealed, and use it to serve and uplift others, thereby helping the human race to evolve. Service and devotion to the Great Work is the shortest road to illumination. The Great Work is the spiritualization of humankind, individually and collectively and the reestablishment of the divinity of humankind.

Kabbalah and Kundalini Yoga

On page 25 is a picture of the Kabbalah Tree of Life. It is a very powerful tool, used by Kabbalists to explain the macrocosm (Universe) and the microcosm (humanity). This symbol is a practical way to understand the Universe, for it displays the immutable laws of nature.

Look at the Tree of Life and you will notice three columns called *pillars*. The pillar on the right is called the *Pillar of Mercy*, which represents the positive male principle. In Kundalini yoga, it relates to the positive mind. The pillar on the left is the *Pillar of Severity*, which is considered to represent the negative female principle. It corresponds to the negative mind. The middle pillar is called the *Pillar of Equilibrium*, and is the balance principle. It relates to the neutral mind, which is ruled by the pituitary and pineal glands. They are called the *divine glands*.

The use of these three aspects of the mind will determine how happy and healthy one can be while on earth. The negative mind is the pillar headed by the planet Saturn. Saturn is the teacher; it allows us to see the obstacles in any situation. The misuse of the negative mind gets us stuck in the loop of fear and insecurity born out of our unpleasant past experiences, especially those from childhood. It keeps us frozen and we cannot properly act. It makes us believe we are losers. By contrast, the positive mind, which is headed by Jupiter, the planet of spiritual and material wellness, makes us see the opportunities in any situation. Jupiter is the planet that makes us happy. In other words, when a person has a positive mental attitude, it is difficult to lose. Finally, the neutral mind, which is ruled by the pituitary and pineal glands, is the path to happiness. The pituitary gland, the most powerful of all chakras, is the seat of intuition. The neutral mind stops impulsive behavior and bestows intuitive logic, which is the highest form of logic and intuition available. With intuition, there is no risk of failure, because it serves the truth and speaks for your highest good. It is accomplished by Kundalini yoga through balancing the five elements in the body, clearing your channels, and opening the chakras, thereby providing you with a very powerful intuition. Intuition is part of the neutral mind. It comes from the pituitary, which is the master gland. Once that gland works properly, one minimizes room for mistakes by intuitively following the laws of nature.

The Tree of Life clearly demonstrates that as long as we live in a physical body, we will be faced by the forces of opposition. Those who experience the right pillar will eventually experience the left pillar, and vice versa.

The Middle Pillar is a way of life that shows us the road to happiness. In the pillar of Equilibrium, the Sun and the Moon are symbolized by the spheres of Tiphareth and Yesod. By properly merging the Sun and the Moon, one connects Malkuth and Kether, which can, respectively, be called Earth and Heaven.

The science of Kundalini yoga is beautifully symbolized by this middle pillar. The way to experience cosmic consciousness is to raise the Kundalini in the body. There are no better ways. Kundalini yoga is the merging of the energy of the Sun with the energy of the Moon, so that the consciousness can rise through the central equilibrium line, which is known in Kabbalah as the Middle Pillar.

Malkuth can be symbolized in Kundalini yoga by the energy located at the navel. The navel is the root of the 72,000 nerves that nourish the whole body with life energy. Therefore, it is a very important point on the body. As Yogi Bhajan teaches, after the eighth year of life, the pineal gland (symbolized by Kether in Kabbalah) no longer fully secretes. It needs to draw from the reserve of energy stored at the navel. In the words of Yogi Bhajan:

> "That energy which developed you and gave you this shape and brought you on this earth has absolutely no residue. It is a pure energy. Do you understand what I am saying? That pure energy is still there. All you have to do is uncoil that energy and make a functional connection with your pineal gland. Once that master gland, the seat of the soul, has started secreting, it will give you the power to reach your self-realization in relationship to the total universal awareness. Scientifically speaking, that is what must happen…"   —from Sadhana Guidelines, page 11

This quote reveals that anyone who practices Kundalini yoga raises his or her frequency, thereby breaking the barrier of limitation created by the mind. As a result, the Universe lifts the veil of ignorance and makes self-realization possible. This quote also helps to show the relation between Kabbalah and Kundalini yoga. Kabbalah can be demonstrated simply by the teachings of this great master, because *the truth is simple.*

In the pillar of Equilibrium, there is an invisible sphere called Daath. It is the door to all knowledge. Daath corresponds on the physical body to the nape of the neck, or *atlas point.* This controls all the various functions related to the neurological system.

Chapter Four

Karma

We are in a period where all the karmic lessons that we have been running away from will come back to seek balance. This is also a time of far-reaching inner transformation and spiritual renewal, where all destructive habits must be replaced by new, healthy ones.

In reality nothing is done by chance and everything follows the karmic laws, some of which are beyond our understanding. It is a well-known cosmic law that everything moves in a circle, and whatever forces we send out into the Universe, will return to us in due course. This is a karmic time, and the Universe is removing the illusions that we have imposed upon ourselves, upon our bodies and upon our realities. It is hard to believe in some unseen laws, in some mysterious cause or power that not only shapes and controls our lives, but also decides on the fate or destiny of even a city or country. During our stay on earth, our thoughts, feelings and actions bring into play the reaction of the laws of nature upon us and everyone in our surroundings.

The Doctrine of Fate relates to the effect of circumstances over which we have no control. We move among invisible forces whose actions we very often do not perceive at all, though we may be profoundly affected by them. There are hundreds of mysteries in life perfectly unknown to humans, beyond our power to analyze and understand.

People often confuse the word fate with destiny. They mean two different things. We have only one destiny; it governs our birthright, which is happiness. Those who follow their hearts or live consciously manifest their destiny, whereas fate is associated with the unhappy side of life. By following the head, being under the influence of a negative ego, or living impulsively, we open the door to the unpleasant influence of fate, which brings pain, suffering, disease or early death.

As the laws which affect the entire Universe affect us, as part of the whole, we also affect those laws and thus one another.

By the application of spiritual work, such as chanting mantra, we bring certain laws into force which react upon time and space so as to surround us with protective and beneficial influences. By practicing with the technology revealed in *Lifting the Veil*, we work on our destiny. As we work on our destiny, so do we raise the consciousness of others. A human who does not know how to seal his aura is susceptible to being at the wrong place in time. We can use our free will and make the choice of either becoming the maker of our destiny or the servant of fate with its painful outcome. We can use the lessons and experiences of the past as the guiding teachers of the present and future.

The way we think, feel, act or speak can help or hinder the state of the world. You generate light by your positive, constructive living and being. There is an old saying, "You need one positive thought to neutralize one hundred negative thoughts." If all of us for seven days put our heart in this experiment, there would be a spiritual transmutation. We need one ray of light to dispel darkness. Our good thoughts, feelings and deeds can illuminate Mother Earth and purify her aura. All our goodness through the positive cosmic laws, can bring such a beneficial collective impact, it will be beyond words to describe. The best and most effective therapy is to create a cause with our thoughts, feelings and actions which is in harmony with the natural laws or the Luminous Forces and Beings of Nature and the whole Universe. We must give absolute priority to this spiritual wisdom which teaches us how to live in harmony with all the spiritual forces and worlds that exist, so that we no longer need to be torn apart by inner conflict and contradiction.

Chapter Five

Principle of Causality

Knock and the door shall be opened unto you.
Seek and ye shall find.
Ask and ye shall be given.
As ye sow, so shall ye reap.

These are four examples of the applications of the Principle of Causality, also known as the law of Cause and Effect. This principle applies to our actions, thoughts and speech but also to the questions we ask of God. When we ask of God, knowledge, sustenance, or direction, we are given that based upon our faith and karma. Our life is continuously in the producing mode. Life is a vibration, meaning up or down. It is energy. It is power. We move and live within this universal creative energy that is life and we cannot prevent it from producing. We can either constructively direct this creative process or we can let it control us. We can determine through our actions what it will bring forth: good or bad; joy or pain, life or death, health or disease. Each of us makes various choices on a daily basis. By doing so, we are using the law of Cause and Effect to build our own pathway to heaven. It is up to us whether we want to make that pathway to heaven smooth and short through positive choices or long and miserable by choosing unwisely.

The law of Cause and Effect is a neutral brush that each of us can use to paint ugly or wonderful pictures in our lives. The use of our free will to direct our thoughts, feelings, speech and deeds, not only plays directly into this law, but it also determines what we ultimately create. God, in his ceaseless effort to be, has given each of us the ability and opportunity to use our free will to direct and channel the universal creative energy both individually and collectively. There are seven major categories of duality that we encounter every single day. These pairs are symbolized by the seven Hebrew double-letters and are represented as follows:

Beth	*Life / Death*
Gimel	*Peace / War*
Daleth	*Wisdom / Foolishness*
Kaph	*Wealth / Poverty*
Peh	*Beauty / Ugliness*
Resh	*Fertility / Sterility*
Tau	*Domination / Dependence*

We all have experiences where utilizing our free will positively results in joy, happiness and health. But there have also been times where unwise choices have caused us to experience mental, emotional and physical pain and health problems. It is the misuse of the law of Cause and Effect which causes some people to be burdened by great sorrows, troubles and dreadful pain. Unfortunately, there are many examples of how just one person's misuse of free will, in the Principle of Causality, can create a chain reaction of pain that affects thousands of people for many generations. However, it only takes one positive use of free will to influence individuals and society.

Physical actions are not the only causes that carry effects. Our unconscious emotions determine who we attract, to what we are attracted, and how we direct our lives. Our emotions may be filled with anger, fear and frustration, or dreams of service, growth and enlightenment. Something you may come across with family, friends and loved ones is the realization that some people unconsciously love fear, anger and insecurity. They are mistrustful of peace and happiness. Therefore, they create a "cause" which makes them seek painful and miserable experiences. They want to affirm their existence through destructive and unhealthy emotions. They only feel alive when they are frustrated and in pain. The only thing that is important to them is the feeling of something wrong. So they go through life trying to create a cause, so as to gather as many destructive experiences as possible.

Until we accept and properly use this Principle of Causality there will continue to be war and disease. Negative thoughts, feelings and deeds are poisonous to our soul and toxic to our physical bodies. It is possible to transmute negativity through the purifying fire of the heart, into the unseen spiritual gold so as to liberate the goodness within us. We can become more conscious by pondering on the causes that created our present situations in life. We should resolve to plant only positive seeds of love and purity in all of our present endeavors and interactions with others.

Kindness, goodness, and compassion lead to happiness and health, because our inner souls are constructed with these qualities. They are the basis for our true nature. They carry the power that not only brings positive transformation, but also shields us from destructive forces. Focus on the good and realize the positive aspects of each situation and harmony will be yours. By concentrating on harmony we are moving away from those negative experiences of life. Through the pure light within us, we can attune ourselves to the higher consciousness that causes us to simply "know" the truth of things. By rising beyond negativity we gain the ability to see the higher manifestations of the universal creative energy in our life.

If you sow criticism, intolerance, selfishness, disloyalty, and negativity, you will not only reap these same qualities, but also, they will be fatal to your health. The practice of racism, gossip, criticism, and bigotry, along with all our vices and passions, actually break the natural laws. These behaviors are contrary to the very structure of our souls, the world and the Universe. They excite the elements and cause catastrophes, disease and trouble of all kinds. Air, fire, water, earth and ether cannot remain harmonious in the presence of anarchy-producing energy. In other words, the elements mimic the state of human behavior and these elements exist in the Universe, on the earth and within our physical bodies. Disease is the state of the elements in the body being out of balance. Just by exhibiting negative behavior, we devastate humankind collectively and individually.

For instance, it is easy for most people to see that the body is a perfect composition of air, fire, water, earth and ether. We have air in our lungs, however air in the wrong area of the body can create disease. The body contains very specific quantities of elements, and any more or less could lead to death. Our body heat is also meant to remain constant within a very narrow scope. The harmony of the five elements in the body is crucial to health. For example, anger, aggression and violence are born out of an imbalance in mental and emotional fire, however this also results in physical imbalances of fire. When communities are plagued by anger, aggression and violence, the collective energy becomes disproportioned and eventually leads to natural disasters, fires and even war. Any element may similarly become imbalanced. Humans must learn that our individual destinies are intricately woven with those of our brothers and sisters, nature, earth and the Universe.

Those who generate destructive energies, inscribe their wickedness into their own spirit. It is known in spiritual circles as the Left or Dark path. Numerous people have injured their health and wealth by either consciously or subconsciously following the Dark path. Remember that bigotry, racism, criticism, superiority complexes and disloyalty are signs of a mind that is easily given to internal or external influences of darkness. This is the road taken by many black magicians which leads straight to the abyss. The very laws of karma and imbalance which they use to sow these malevolent energies, will teach them through painful experiences, and finally shake them out of darkness. To change evil or darkness in mankind we first have to change evil or darkness in ourselves. We have to make up our mind to be good and kind.

Focus on the good and realize the positive aspects of each situation, and harmony and health will be yours.

We must remember that things done cannot be undone. They can never be annihilated. Each of our thoughts, speech and deeds become a part of the Akashic record that can never be erased and will follow us to infinity. It is you who makes your life choices. You are accountable for each one. There should be a sublime joy in taking responsibility for our life, because when we are truly able to comprehend the causes behind the choices we make, we will have learned the most important key to a joyful and productive life.

Humankind can direct the law of Cause and Effect in order to sow goodness for all. By sowing blessings, we become blessed. By sowing good, we get goodness. By giving thanks we open the heart and receive more. The more thankful we are, the more blessed we become. The more grateful we feel, the more good we attract. We will be blessed with more grace and prosperity based upon how grateful we are for the little or big things we have already received. Thus, anything we bless and are thankful and grateful for will multiply. If we complain about challenges and fill our days with curses and regret, those too will multiply. Making the choice between the two is a personal matter. Although it is easy for most humans to always be critical and see the negative in every situation, one must practice gratitude and take time to recognize the positive in order to create a better life.

Individually and collectively, the call of duty is to help raise the vibration of the Earth by creating good causes. With good thinking, feeling, speech and deeds we create causes which produce good experiences. By creating good experiences we purify the Akashic Record instead of polluting it with negative actions. By generating causes through positive thoughts, feelings, and deeds we will receive beneficial influences from the luminous beings who love us and watch our every step. Therefore, we must raise the vibration around us and lift the light of spirit in order to make other people's lives better. We need to raise our frequency to the highest vibrational waves of consciousness possible and live life from that place. We should live our lives from the highest vibration of consciousness we are capable of in order to face the challenges of time and space with grace. We must avoid living life in the lowest frequencies of trouble and misery. By doing this, we are acting selfishly from within and reacting to outside influences. The way we choose to react is our chance to raise our vibration, share our gifts with the Universe, and shine our light onto others. *grace* .

The Power of Words

Before you speak, remember that God sits at the tip of your tongue. It takes one right word to generate a cause whose effect can move a life in trouble in the right direction, bringing joy and happiness. But it also takes one wrong word to cause damage, pain and suffering that lasts a lifetime. There have been people who have said wrong things during a moment of fear, insecurity or anger. These words which become recorded, not only expose their personality core, but also, come back to hurt them or destroy friendship and love. One should not speak in anger. In anger or fear you do not speak consciously, because you are not yourself. When you speak consciously, your consciousness and what you say are favored by the Universe. Those who abuse the power of the word, and have made destroying others their life's work, will have to pay for it sooner or later. There is no way around it.

SPIRITUAL NONSENSE

There are spiritual people who meditate for hours a day to improve their lives and get close to God, then turn around to criticize, gossip and hate others. Ironically, the same people cannot understand why nothing works in their lives, especially when they are faced with serious health troubles. The only person you can fool is yourself, not the Universe to whom you are transparent. If you meditate for one or more hours a day to merge with God and have a good life, then turn around to destroy someone's reputation by spreading dirt on their name, your affairs will not work. This is the same as someone taking a pill for a headache and then hitting their head against a wall. Why take the pill?

You can injure someone in various ways. When you use your words to kill another's good name and reputation, it is like slowly murdering the person with a knife. We cannot take back what we say; we have no power over our words after they have left our lips. They become Akashic record and will come back to haunt us to infinity.

You must be both compassionate and tolerant and maintain your humanness. Claiming to love God and turning around to hate, criticize and gossip is spiritual nonsense. God is in everyone, so as a spiritual person, you must see God in each person that you may want to criticize.

The effect of your spiritual practices are either enhanced or reduced by your pattern of speech, your thoughts and actions. It is the combination of the above that creates the experiences of your life. If you happen to be the focus of such negative criticism and gossip, I would suggest that you merge with God, raise your frequency and expand your light. Bless and pray for those who are spreading unhealthy vibrations about you, and let the Universe take over. Soon you will see that darkness cannot stand before the power of light. Others will witness with amazement, the grace, protection and divinity of God manifesting in your life.

Gossip, hatred and criticism are the way of darkness. They weaken the aura and attract misfortune. No one can get away from their effects. Positive speech brings good luck, because words have the power to create our reality. Stay away from those who destroy others with their words if you cannot change them, so that your energy field may not be contaminated by their dirt. Anything that comes out of your mouth should uplift, not destroy. That is the spiritual way—the way of the light.

Those who criticize and hate have triggered the karmic force of punishment with their destructive thoughts, feelings, speech and deeds. There is a basic spiritual law of balance: everything a victimizer wishes for or does to an innocent victim will be fulfilled onto himself in this life or another. Eventually, in subsequent rebirth, their spirit reawakens. They repent of their envious actions, they reform and are graduated from their incarnation so that they can continue their true life until their ultimate liberation from the cycles of life and death.

Those who, out of jealousy and envy, use lies, gossip, criticism, and negativity to destroy others or demean their talent, are only destroying themselves, for what you send out, inevitably, returns to you a hundred fold. Many good people have been destroyed through the ill will of others, because they allowed themselves to be victimized. They believed and accepted other people's destructive remarks about them. If you find yourself in this case, know that you are a spiritual being and nothing can stop the unfoldment of your good except your lack of faith in God. Open yourself to God's light, and let it fill you with unlimited strength. Let it surround you with protection. Think, feel, and align yourself with light. Let that light shine in all of your affairs and dispel any darkness generated by negativity. Never lose heart. Trust your spiritual force and pray, because prayer transforms all misfortunes into delight.

Peace is found more often in patience than
in judgment hence it is better that we should be
accused unjustly than that we should accuse others,
even in justice. The more we advance in virtue,
the less we perceive the defects of others.
As a man on the summit of the mountain with
a vast prospect about him, beholds not the deformities
of those who may dwell on the plain below.
His very elevation should give him a lively
and tender interest in those who, although beneath him
are, he knows, of his own nature.
What then must be the love of God for men.

—Louis Claude St. Martin

Chapter Six

The Sun and the Moon

The heavens are changing, the Earth is changing, and we are changing. Humankind has come to a crossroad in our evolution where all the karmic lessons we have been running away from are coming back to seek balance. This is also a time of far-reaching inner transformation and spiritual renewal, where all destructive habits must be replaced with constructive ones. This is not the time to let the ego spend its wealth and power to isolate us. Rather, it is the time to identify with our higher Self, so as to experience our oneness with all. It is time for us to learn, understand, honor and obey the immutable laws of nature, so that we may experience and support the cosmic flow and harmony of life. It is now time for our expanded Self to become the custodian of the heavenly light and use the knowledge of Kabbalah and yoga to experience the vastness of our identity and to serve a greater cause. The only way to release our fear, anger, doubt, insecurities and pain is by developing a relationship with our expanded identity. The only way to conquer our destructive patterns is by aligning with our spirit, and the only way to feel comfortable is by learning the divine spiritual wisdom, so we can experience our totality. Our challenge in this age is to forgive others and ourselves and to expand our experience of Self and life.

Time and space have changed. We have moved from the age of darkness and ignorance into a time of light and awareness. Light is knowledge and ignorance is darkness. You can hide things in the darkness, but light reveals all. This is a time of high vibrational heart energy. The Aquarian Age does not tolerate ignorance. It is a time of spirituality, forgiveness, and no secrets.

The Earth, too, is undergoing a major transformation of consciousness. This new energy makes everything in the lives of those who are currently living on Earth shift very quickly. This new energy can be witnessed in the realm of technology—for as a result of computers and the internet, people are being massively inundated with information, both valuable and useless. As this energy gathers momentum, the human nervous system will be bombarded and shattered by the stress of an overload of information. Our free will is going to be severely tested in its power of choice, as it was in the Garden of Eden, before the fall of Adam and Eve. The misuse of free will in this age will be both unwise and very costly, for making mistakes at the wrong time can potentially destroy one's whole life.

It is vital to be in harmony with the unseen forces that direct our lives, and if not, life can feel like a struggle. In the past, it was easier to get away with not living in accordance with the laws of nature, but this will no longer work. A good analogy to this is driving a car and consistently running red lights in traffic. One may get away with it for a while, but eventually it catches up with you, either in the form of a costly ticket or worse, a deadly accident. Now, more than ever, we must live in harmony with the laws of nature, for this is the road to peace and happiness. But in order to live in harmony with the laws of nature, one must know the laws of the Universe. Therefore, it is essential to learn to see the unseen and know the unknown.

Remember there are two worlds: the one we see, or the visible, material world, and the one we do not see, the invisible, immaterial world. From the teachings of Yogi Bhajan, we learn that the visible world represents only ten percent of what is here, and the invisible world consists of the other ninety percent. Yet ironically, we rely ninety percent on what we see and only ten percent on the unseen. The fact is, our lives are basically ruled by unseen forces, because the invisible supports the visible. Therefore, it is in our best interest to understand the unseen forces behind the major rhythms of nature. In doing so, we can learn how to be at the right place at the right time, thus creating the best possible outcome. Success is in the timing!

Therefore, seeking assistance from the Sun and the Moon in any endeavor cannot be overemphasized. The Sun and the Moon are two visible forces that we can strongly relate to. For example, on sunny days, we can feel the joy that the energy of the Sun brings. Everyone receives its warming and enlivening rays. Anytime the day is overcast, most people's moods are affected. Everything looks gray and lifeless. When the Sun suddenly appears and the clouds begin to disperse, we feel a presence of life. Try to imagine the Sun's sheer magnificence. It showers the Earth with more energy each hour than we can truly comprehend. The Sun is about 860,000 miles in diameter and around 108 times larger than the Earth. It is 92,900,000 miles away from the earth. The average surface temperature is about 10,832° fahrenheit. The fact is, there would be no life on earth if it was not for the Sun showering us with the pranic life-force. This clearly indicates the power of the Sun in our lives.

The sacred teachings of Kabbalah can no longer remain hidden, because they are greatly needed at this time. This is one of the reasons why Kabbalah is now being studied by more people than ever before. Although the outer teachings of Kabbalah are being revealed to the masses, you must look for the inner teachings. For this you must look to the Sun. Most people have not yet realized that the Sun is a source of power that can work for us. Most of the ancient tribes in all recorded history venerated the Sun more highly than we currently do. Some of those civilizations devoted almost their entire accumulated wealth to building and decorating temples, and even holy cities, to the worship of this "fire of heaven." Even the Egyptians revered the Sun, which they referred to as *Ra*. Working with the Sun is the highest practice of Kabbalah. It will give you understanding of the mysteries of life and show you the splendor of the inner Kabbalah, which reveals the secrets of heaven and earth.

The Sun is a source of energy, life and warmth. The essence of the holy Kabbalah and source of all spirituality is in the Sun. The Sun is the eye of God, and the eyes are the window of our soul. Therefore, you can connect with the soul of God through the Sun. The Sun is a striking visible representation of God on Earth. Thus, it is the fountain of light and a visible representation of spirit in action. Joy, peace and love are the attributes of light. Confusion, suffering and disease are attributes of duality. There is no reality in duality. Reality is only found in divinity or oneness. The Sun is the doorway to divinity. The simple act of focusing the mind on the Sun creates oneness on the spot. Since the Sun is reflected in our heart center, allowing the mind to contemplate the Sun opens our heart center, thereby facilitating the experience of elevation in consciousness. If you keep up with this process, one day the Sun will rise in your heart.

The Sun is the mathematical center of our solar system and all the planets spin around it with absolute harmony. In other words, it is the heart of our Universe. In Kabbalah, the sphere that corresponds with the Sun is located exactly at the center of the Tree of Life.

The fact that the Sun is the doorway to universal awareness can be Kabbalistically explained by the following: If you observe the Tree of Life, you will notice that Tiphareth, which is associated with the Sun, has been attributed to the number six descending from the top. Six stands for the Star of David. Adding up all the numbers contained in 6 $(1+2+3+4+5+6)$ gives us 21. The reduction of 21 $(2+1)$ equals 3—the number of divinity. Another addition of the numbers in 3 $(1+2+3)$ will give us 6. By repeating the same process, you will realize that Tiphareth of the Sun (6) brings you divinity (3). In other words, we can experience elevation of consciousness by working on Tiphareth within us.

The energy of this age is at the level of Tiphareth, which is located at the mathematical center of the Tree of Life. Tiphareth stands for the Sun; it also represents the heart center. The heart center is situated in the middle of the seven chakras; it is the balance point in the body. In other words, our heart center is a reflection of the Sun in us. This is the center of higher consciousness where experiences from all our incarnations are recorded. It is the location of our higher Self—the part of us that does not die with physical death and lasts for as long as it takes for us to be liberated from the cycle of life and death. Our lower self—symbolized by the three spiritual centers located below the chest—only lasts one lifetime.

Upon death, the Sun in us, our higher Self, records the essence of all our experiences and sends a projection of itself into the world to balance our incurred debts.

The heart chakra is the center for healing and balance, through which you can fulfill your nature and express your soul. To be in harmony with the Aquarian Age, you have to follow your heart, otherwise you will suffer. Many people do not live from the heart, for they are too busy with their heads. In this age, humanity shall both come from the heart and shine like the Sun. Teachings of truth will open your heart, thereby removing fear and obsession with control, and making you compassionate and tolerant. Opening your heart will harmonize you with this age, so you can experience health, happiness and holiness.

It is through the heart that you can manifest your highest destiny. Therefore, by relating to the Sun, it will rise in your heart and the Universe will assist you in all your endeavors. As Kabbalists, yogis or spiritual practitioners, if you want to have a deeper understanding of life, you must model yourself on the Sun. The best way to know God is through the Sun. The light of the Sun is the living spirit. By working with the Sun, all the dormant qualities and virtues in you are brought to full life and start producing beautiful deeds. Like the Sun, you will be able to warm and light up everyone you meet, touch or speak to.

By raising our consciousness to the Sun, we create a positive condition in our lives, which inspires, strengthens and heals. You rise above all mundane manifestations, and thus are impregnated by the highest quality, and filled with peace, harmony and love. Your solar plexus and sympathetic nervous system automatically get charged with light, thereby making you tireless and full of vitality.

A spiritual law states that whatever you relate to, you become. By relating to the Sun, one becomes like the Sun. Those who meditate on the Sun not only develop the ability to serve and uplift others, but also radiate tremendous personal magnetism. To become a true servant of the Universe, you must relate to the Sun. By doing so, you will possess the glory of the brightness of the whole world, and all darkness will disappear from your life. Those who understand the light of the Sun, emanate a beautiful solar radiance and light that everyone they meet cannot help but acknowledge. The Sun will give you the elevation of spirit to gracefully overcome the challenges of time and space.

The Sun serves, heals and uplifts us all. It is time for humanity to serve and uplift others. Bear in mind that God serves those who serve others. By uplifting others, you attract the grace of God in your life. Living like the Sun generates high vibrational energy, creating speedy and powerful changes in your mental, spiritual and physical being. The way of the Sun creates high vibration. Negativity cannot remain in the presence of high vibration.

Please do not get caught in any Kabbalah group that makes you develop a superiority complex and leads you to believe you belong to the chosen few. This is not a good karma to carry; it is one for which you inevitably will have to pay. Whether we like it or not, we are all interconnected. It is by working together that we can all make it. No one will be saved until all are saved. When you work with the Sun, you become a universal Kabbalist—one who is ageless, raceless, classless and genderless, who sees God in all, who knows that everyone is a ray of the Sun.

I would like to add a word of wisdom. Now that Kabbalah is becoming popularized, you must be aware of the following. In our world of duality, there is a positive and negative aspect to absolutely everything. Technology, for instance, when utilized for positive purposes, is very beneficial, but when misused, can lead to mass destruction. Similarly, there is a light side and a dark side to Kabbalah. By working with the Sun, you are practicing the Kabbalah of light. The Sun is the fountain of light, and where there is light you cannot find darkness. One of the reasons Kabbalah was kept secret for so many years was to ensure the proper application of this knowledge, and avoid repeating what happened during the Egyptian civilization. The Egyptians were versed in both the Kabbalah of light and the Kabbalah of darkness. The fall of the Egyptian empire was a direct result of the abuse of the dark side of Kabbalah. Therefore, the safest and most effective form of Kabbalah is universal Kabbalah, which is the way of the Sun. Work with the Sun and let its light be your shield, for the

Universe supports those who work with light. Practice Kabbalah of the Sun in the spirit of love and light to heal yourself and uplift others.

 ## MEDITATING ON THE SUN: INCREASE AND SPREAD YOUR LIGHT

Meditating on the psychic Sun will connect you to your higher Self. It will open your heart and bring you happiness. It is a practice which positively strengthens the life-force in the body, resulting in improved health and well-being on all levels. Meditating on the Sun attracts good fortune, including all of the good things that this life has to offer. By doing this meditation, your light will contribute in serving all those who suffer or who need any aid whatsoever.

POSITION

Sit in a comfortable, meditative position, either sitting on a mat or pillow with legs crossed or on a chair with feet flat on the ground. The spine is straight. Close your eyes and take 3 long deep breaths.

VISUALIZATION

Mentally lift your consciousness from your body and go in spirit to the Sun. Enter into its blazing aura and proceed to the body of the Sun itself. Have no fear. You are a child of the Sun and this is your rightful home. Allow the Sun's tremendous energy to flow through your entire being, invigorating and strengthening every particle in you. Visualize yourself surrounded by the warm and healing light. Now visualize the earth and send your most positive loving and healing thoughts through the rays of the Sun towards the earth.

RECITE THE FOLLOWING PRAYER

By reciting the prayer of light daily, you automatically become a benefactor of humankind. By projecting the words of love, peace and light you are sending out constructive healing vibrations of light to help, uplift, enlighten and heal others. The prayer of love, peace and light makes you work in the light for the light.

(continued on next page)

Love before me
Love behind me
Love at my left
Love at my right
Love above me
Love below me
Love unto me
Love in my surroundings
Love to all
Love to the Universe

Peace before me
Peace behind me
Peace at my left
Peace at my right
Peace above me
Peace below me
Peace unto me
Peace in my surroundings
Peace to all
Peace to the Universe

Light before me
Light behind me
Light at my left
Light at my right
Light above me
Light below me
Light unto me
Light in my surroundings
Light to all
Light to the Universe

The Moon

The Moon is a small planet—only 2,160 miles in diameter—but because it is so close to us, its effects on the Earth and those who live upon it are vast. The Moon influences us more than any other planet aside from the Sun, for her vibrations are felt from the tides of the ocean to the waves of the human mind. Since our bodies are composed of about seventy-five to eighty percent liquid, it follows that the Moon, which moves and influences the Earth's oceans, also moves and greatly influences the human body.

The Sun is a visible representation of the masculine principle of God, whereas the Moon is a visible representation of the feminine aspect of God. The Moon plays the role of the Mother, and the Sun of the Father. The Moon rules water, and its action is described as fluctuating, changeable, absorbent and receptive.

The Moon is also the great magnet of nature, exerting a magnetic influence upon this planet many times more powerful than that of all the other planets put together. This force lifts and holds erect all the organic life upon the surface of the planet. It is the Moon's ability to balance the pull of the Earth that causes all organic liquids to be held in suspension. If it were not for the Moon, all moist organisms would simply collapse, sucked flat by terrestrial gravity.

The lunar force sustains the millions of separate magnetic fields which animate all individual living bodies upon Earth. Every living organism endowed with the life that comes from the Sun, constitutes such an individual and ephemeral magnetic field. Although life comes from the Sun, it is the Moon which transmutes the positive ions of the Sun into life-giving negative ions.

Every soul who comes to Earth must pass through the Moon, as every child must come through his or her mother. The nine months spent in the womb respectively correspond to following planets: Saturn, Jupiter, Mars, Sun, Venus, Mercury, Moon, Saturn and Jupiter. The Moon symbolizes the astral light which contains the five elements of ether, air, fire, water and earth. The human body is composed of these five elements, and at death, decomposes back into them. Thus human souls come through and exit through the Moon.

The human capacity to move the limbs is due to the influence of the Moon. The Sun rules the heart, and the heart acts as a built-in pump that keeps the blood system in constant circulation against the terrestrial and lunar pulls. And it is the Moon which maintains the lymph system in suspension, allowing it to interact with the other by osmosis. The Moon gives one the ability to move, and that movement renews the lymph circulation. This circulation is essential, for it cleanses the body and rids it of poisons. The lack of circulation can create a gradual accumulation of toxins, eventually leading to unbearable muscular pain.

Since the body is up to eighty percent water and the Moon rules water, by working with it, you can control eighty percent of your health. That is why the first thing one should do when faced with health challenges is work with the Moon on a physical and spiritual level. The Moon on a physical level is represented by water and the drinking of it can cleanse the system, for water is the mother of life, and through it we can contact the pure energy of the Universe. One particularly effective way of benefiting from the healing energy of water is by sipping it slowly. On the spiritual level the Moon is accessed by breathing through just the left nostril. Left-nostril breathing brings lunar energy into the body. Left-nostril breathing renews the blood, sharpens intuition and enhances overall health. *(See meditation "Immune System Booster" in Chapter Nine/Sun Period.)*

The Moon exerts much influence on the psychic activity of humans. In astrology the Moon represents the imaginative and reflective side of a person and is linked to the subconscious mind. The Moon rules the pituitary gland, master of the glandular system, which in turn is linked to the akashic record—the part of the collective psyche where everything that has ever been is recorded. Actually the Moon center, or pituitary gland controls the whole reproductive process. Our sexual force constitutes ninety percent of our immune system energy, and that force is ruled by the Moon.

The mastery of that force can contribute to spiritual growth. Conversely, the misuse of Moon or sexual energy can potentially be detrimental to our health. By a wise use or conservation of the sexual energy, we charge our blood with pranic force, improve our health, and stimulate our spiritual body by activating the psychic centers through yoga and meditation. The Moon not only relates to the physical reproductive system, it also is linked to the mental ability to reproduce or materialize desires, for the lunar force symbolizes the mental ability to create and project a thought form into a visible and tangible manifestation.

The Moon corresponds to the sphere *Yesod* which stands for foundation. It also relates to the tarot card the High Priestess which represents fluctuation, change and perception of high truths, symbolized by the principle of cause and effect.

The Moon follows a 28 day cycle—the time it takes for it to travel around the Earth, at an average distance of 250,000 miles. In those 28 days the Moon goes through all the influences that the Sun goes through in 365 days. Those 28 days are divided into phases which influence everything on planet Earth, from the vegetable kingdom to the animal world, including man. Therefore, it is vital that you work with the Moon, and make it your clock.

THE PHASES OF THE MOON

When the Moon is in conjunction with the Sun, it is called a new Moon. When the Sun and Moon are in opposition, it is called a full Moon. By following the phases of the Moon, and working with the tides, you can find fortune and success in all your endeavors. In other words, you can easily reach your destination and improve your affairs by making better use of the tides. As said earlier, the Moon, being closest to the earth, not only influences the tides and plant growth, but man's affairs as well. Most people have a tendency to discount its effects. Anyone who takes the phases of the Moon into consideration in any spiritual operation will have nothing but success.

The waxing Moon lasts about two weeks—starting from the new Moon up to the day before the full Moon. This is when the tides are most favorable for spiritual and material expansion. It is the most propitious time to get married, start a new job, begin any productive project, or acquire a new pet. Anything started in that period will grow beautifully. Plants respond to the phases of the Moon; therefore the best time to plant a garden is during the waxing period.

The first part of the waxing moon, from the new moon to the seventh day is the first quarter. This first quarter is an especially potent time for a new start, particularly on the night showing the first tiny sliver of the new Moon. The second quarter, from the eighth day to the to the day before the full Moon is also a beneficial time for starting constructive activities, sowing, planting, initiating new ventures, investments and inauguration of personal relationships.

The time from the full Moon to the day before the new Moon is the waning period. The waning Moon also lasts about two weeks. This is the most advantageous period to remove unwanted things from your life. For example, it is the best time to get rid of diseases that have been ailing you. Therefore, start the healing process when the Moon is descending. This is the best time for reaping of crops, cleaning out your closets, extermination of pests and parasites, surgical removal of growths, etc... The waning moon is not the best time to get married, because its not a good time to start things. The waning period is also not the best time to do work of Light. You will find that most acts of black magic are performed during this period.

Interestingly, the light of the Moon is known to impact the growth of medicinal plants, which grow faster at night, under the moonlight. Also, the changes of the Moon affect certain people more than others, for example, those who are mentally unstable, as well as people who carry a lot of water in their body.

During the full Moon, animals, birds and reptiles are much more active and restless than they are during the rest of the lunar cycle. Major mystical operations are conducted during certain phases of the Moon, and the full Moon is the most potent time for spiritual work.

There are four powerful days in the 28-day cycle of the Moon which can be used to improve your health. These days are the new Moon, full Moon, and the tenth and eleventh days of the Moon. Each phase of the Moon has a specific effect on the integral workings of the body. For example, the eleventh day of the Moon cycle is the optimum day to influence the glandular system. On that day, the glands are the most susceptible to being cleansed and stimulated, so it is an optimum day to give your body a break and fast.

Combining fasting with meditation is a sure way to advance spiritual development. These powerful days of the Moon cycle generate a certain kind of pressure on the endocrine system, so that it can secrete and cleanse itself. Fasting on these particular days is the best thing you can do for your health and healing, for it is a great therapy. Fasting is a powerful way to restore and maintain the body's natural equilibrium. In fact, you can strengthen your immune system and remove many illnesses through proper fasting.

The position of the Moon in relationship to the Sun and the Earth creates varied magnetic fields. As mentioned earlier, the various stages of the Moon influence man and nature in various ways. By synchronizing your body with the lunar cycle, you are harmonizing with the natural healing rhythm of our solar system. So, if you can train your body to automatically tune into the Moon cycle, the lunar energies will help cleanse, purify, strengthen and empower you in return.

 FULL MOON
MEDITATION

Here is a full Moon meditation. By honestly practicing it, you will
harmonize yourself with the Universe, thereby creating room for a
holy, happy and healthy life.

POSITION

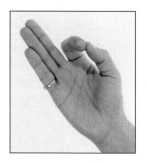

1. Sit in a meditative position.

2. With your spine straight, apply neck
   lock, by pulling in your chin.

3. Your hands are resting on your knees
   in Gyan mudra, with your index and
   thumbtips touching.

4. Your eyes are one-tenth open, focused at the end of your nose.

5. Your teeth are locked firmly together and the underside
   of your tongue is pressed to the roof of your mouth.

MENTAL FOCUS

Mentally project SA-TA-NA-MA from the point between your
brows, which is also known as the third eye.

> *SA* is existence
> *TA* is life
> *NA* is death
> *MA* is rebirth

TIME

Continue for 15–90 minutes.

Chapter Seven

Prosperity

Success, wealth and material abundance do not come by chance. Rather, wealth is the result of the effect which you yourself have instituted. For it is what you think, feel, say, do, and believe, that makes you what you are tomorrow, next month and next year. Those are the things that combine to make up your karma, and the quality of your livelihood is determined by your positive and negative karmic influences. Your present conditions are either the punishment or the reward for your behavior in your previous lives. Your current life is only a journey that is preparing you for another future existence. Just as today is the outcome of yesterday, you create your tomorrow from today. Opportunity is not a thing which fate provides; it is something created by humans themselves. A man can only reap what he sows.

There is material richness and material poverty, spiritual richness and spiritual poverty, wealth of knowledge and ignorance. They each not only teach lessons, but also, they give you a chance to burn karma.

Everything in the Universe, including material richness, is ruled by a particular universal law. Mastery of the laws of nature causes you to overcome limitations and succeed in life. An understanding of universal laws can assist you in improving the quality of your livelihood. These laws are there to prevent chaos and maintain the order and principle of balance that keeps life itself going.

Without spiritual wisdom money can turn a human into a beast and bring out the worst in a person. Material richness or wealth corresponds to the earth or fire triangle of the Star of David with the apex pointing up. Very often, wealth without spiritual wisdom is a curse. It releases the unfettered and dangerous energies of the inferior astral world which progressively attracts the destructive forces of nature. It causes the fire of sex, money and power to gradually eat one alive. It takes away peace of mind and affects one's mental, emotional and physical health. One needs the heavenly or water triangle to balance the energy of money. Wealth along with spiritual wisdom is a blessing. It creates in a person's life the perfect manifestation of the Star of David—two interlaced triangles—bestowing upon one divine grace and peace.

It is very difficult to meditate when you are confronted with outstanding debts, especially when you don't know where the next dollar is coming from. As a spiritual person, whether money is important to you or not, the continuous lack of it in your life may reveal your misunderstanding of reality and spirituality. You came on this earth as a spiritual being to have a human experience. You are not a human being having a spiritual experience. You are not going to tell your bill collectors when the payment is due that you are spiritual. In our present society, exchange is measured by money. Earning a living, paying your bills and facing your responsibilities are part of being spiritual. This is another way of playing your part in the evolution of the human race.

Cooperation with the laws of nature combined with hard work and perseverance can be used to reverse poverty. We can acquire wealth by making the best possible use of the tools life gives us. Our understanding of reality is determined by how money flows in and out of our life. Money is there to help us create a better world. It is a useful tool that allows us to multiply our opportunities for ourselves and others, improve our lives, and provide us with freedom and time needed to devote to our relationships, personal development and spiritual growth. Your level of consciousness determines the amount of money the Universe gives you. Richness comes from finding ways to improve the quality of life for yourself and others.

Any wealth, whether it be spiritual, financial, or intellectual must be used for the good of humankind.

It is important to keep in mind that the Universe will give you anything that you ask for and need, but you must deserve it. In the same way, you cannot expect to be paid for a job you have not done. No one can receive what they have not merited in this life or other incarnations. One earns a thing one needs, when one obtains it through one's own effort. Nothing can be gained without the sacrifice of something else. When we don't know what we want we become incapable of promoting our own livelihood. When your goals are clear, you are suddenly able to stop wasting energy on choosing a direction. You can begin to pluck available opportunities from each moment like ripe oranges from a tree. Time, will, and energy can be wisely transmuted to obtain health and/or money. But there must be a balance here, because when more time than is required is invested to acquire wealth, your mental, emotional and/or physical health suffer.

When people attempt to get what they have not earned or deserved in this life or other incarnations, they violate the universal law of balance and order. When people break the law of harmony or cheat to obtain something, they suffer a loss in this life or another, equal to what was unfairly taken. When something is yours, nobody can take it away from you. When it is time to let go of something, holding onto to it can be detrimental to your spiritual growth and health.

Do not envy those who seem to be eating with a golden spoon or living rich lives. Life, in all its winding paths, has many pitfalls, even for those who appear to be well off. Never envy the destiny of others. They are pilgrims on the journey of life, the same as all humans. We do not know what severe trials may await them tomorrow, or through what rough seas of sorrow they have sailed in their past. Appearances are deceiving. Judgments that are made too quickly do a spiritual disservice to both the envious and the envied.

We must also remember that no one is immune to downfall. On
the contrary, the higher up we are, the more we must invest in the
flow of life to create abundance. The peak always signals the beginning of the valley. The lowest point means we're beginning to climb
again. By investing in spiritual wisdom we create a buffer which
warms our heart and protects us by absorbing any disturbances
created by the wheel of fortune.

To reverse poverty you must realize and believe with your whole
heart that you are valuable, that you have a bottomless well of end-
less personal gifts to share with the Universe. Few self-made men
have had any education. Many highly educated men are poor.
Improvement can be made everywhere. Every man is a gold mine to
himself, and instead of letting others exploit you, exploit yourself.

Become the best or highest you can ever be in your calling, for the
best in you is light, it is God. When you strive to become the best
you can be in your calling, your work becomes a vocation. Your daily
life becomes healing to every human soul and numerous opportunities for wealth appear to you from unexpected places. By bringing the
best out of yourself, you create a spiritual barrier against poverty.
Make it a point to know your business from top to bottom. Those
who are the best in their field always have more work than they can
handle. Being the best you can be in your field of endeavor gives you
the self-confidence of a leader to whom people are naturally
attracted. Wealth goes to those who trust themselves. Create opportunity by having belief in yourself. Every human being is born with
a gift that can contribute to a positive evolution of humankind.

Poverty comes from an impotency of the human will power, an
inability to learn a quantitative and qualitative amount of knowledge
in your calling, combined with an ignorance of the laws of nature.
Poverty is a condition of disharmony. Poverty is repelled by people
who are willing to learn, and it is attracted to those who place their
trust in other persons. In astrology, there are squares and trines.
Trines are signs of happiness and flow, and squares are signs of sad-

ness and challenge. When your karma locks you in a square, causing you bad luck and poverty, you can use your knowledge of the laws of nature, along with a strong and wisely directed will-energy to cut the square diagonally, making it a double trine. A double trine brings double luck and happiness.

Of course, modern life is expensive. Most of our money is spent on bills, rent, and basic living expenses. But remember, the Universe is divided into ten regions or Sephiroth. From one, Kether gave rise to other spheres until the ten emanations were created. These emanations represent the pattern of the Universe. Therefore to be in harmony with the Universe divide your earnings into ten parts like the ten regions of the Universe. The first tenth pay to God or a place or organization that nourishes you spiritually such as your church, synagogue, temple, etc,. This divine and timeless act unifies you with the Universe, opening within and without an inflow and outflow of the Universe's bounty. It also burns karma and removes misfortune. By tithing to the source of the teachings that nourish and sustain you, you will receive a host of blessings and benefits. When you give willingly to the higher consciousness that directs and protects you in whatever form that may take, you open yourself to receive more.

The second tenth pay to yourself in the form of savings and investment. From this tenth is the seed from which your tree of wealth shall grow. And the more faithfully you nourish and water that tree with constant savings, the sooner may you bask in the contentment beneath its shade. Every amount of money you save is a slave to work for you. This money also will have its own children who are waiting to work for you.

The remaining should be used to support your livelihood and well-being. We have a tendency to have eyes bigger than our stomachs. We often want more than we can afford and more than we actually need. The desires we gratify should only be those that are truly essential.

Money always attracts opportunities, out of which nine tenths are no good. Therefore, multiply your savings by putting it in a profitable investment. This is one aspect of the law of the Ten-fold System. Wealth loves those who work with a system. Keep in mind that money is only a tool. People should not be judged by their material success, their financial wealth, or by the beautiful objects that they may have acquired. They should be judged by their spiritual and moral worth, by the gifts they share with the world, and the love that lives in their hearts. Spiritual worth is the only lasting wealth.

The Art of Attracting Green Energy

There is no pleasure on the earth that can possibly match spiritual joy. There is no joy like that which comes from wisdom. When a human truly experiences the pleasures which come from spirituality, he/she no longer has a taste for anything else. Developing one's spiritual nature is the ultimate peace-giving and inspiring practice which fills the heart with true happiness and joy while improving one's health. All other pleasures are not only temporary, but also keep the heart restless and fill life with emptiness, whereas spiritual pleasure keeps the heart full with the light of healing joy. When a person invests in spiritual wisdom, it takes such good care of him that it turns even his misfortune into delight.

All true servants of the Universe for whom livelihood is not guaranteed depend on divine collaboration to see them through the challenges of time and space. They understand what it means to really trust God and make room in their life for his light to illuminate and nourish them. The Universe always takes care of its agents of light. In my modified version of how one mystic puts it, God always serves those who serve others. For there is no power, either of ether, air, fire, water and earth, or scourge of God, which is not obedient to the necessity of the servant of the Universe. As an extension of God, that which he has, he has not. But that which he is, he is and that which he will be, he will be. And neither God, nor man, nor all the fallen angels, can either check him or cause him to waver for one instant upon the path. This command and this promise have been given to all true servants of the Universe, without exception.

In Matthew 6, verse 33, it has been promised "But seek ye first the kingdom of God, and his righteousness; and all these things shall be added unto you." By learning the laws of the Universe, developing our spiritual nature and putting God first, we attract the good graces of the Universe, causing our rightful wishes to be fulfilled.

It is in the very actions of seeking the kingdom of God and understanding the laws of nature that brings us into harmony with the Universe. Our spiritual action brings grace and divinity into our lives, and we become deserving of the divine grace being granted to us. However, if we give up our search for God and turn our backs away from him, refusing to believe in the existence of a supreme spiritual being, we disengage ourselves from the helpful influences of heaven. By accepting the presence and believing sincerely in the spiritual forces existing in the Universe and within ourselves, we bring into action the creative forces of the Universe to work for and with us.

Start each day by giving thanks for what you have already received and give thanks for the opportunities that lie ahead. This active appreciation brings about a continuous strengthening of the harmonious relationship we have established with the spiritual forces within us. One of the most powerful ways to bring prosperity into your life is to bless everything and give thanks for everything, because everything you bless and give thanks for increases. By practicing gratitude and blessing, you put into practice one of the greatest laws of prosperity and plenty. For with thankfulness and blessings comes increase. The law of gratitude for everything is a fundamental spiritual law.

Your level of consciousness determines the amount of money the Universe gives you. It will be given unto you by measure of your faith. Expect your every need to be met. Expect the answer to every problem. Expect abundance on every level. As you expect the very best in life, you draw it to you. Correspondingly, if you expect the best in others, it will be drawn from them. So start right now expecting the very best in everything and everyone and watch the very best come about.

Our actions of seeking heaven and harmonizing ourself with the spiritual powers and principles of the Universe will fill our lives with grace and blessings of all kinds and take care of all our needs.

More on Green Energy

Green is the color of prosperity. Allow me to explain. From an early age, the Universe has blessed me with the wisdom of the Kabbalah and a thorough understanding of the science of divination. As a result, I have met people of all walks of life, from the poorest to the richest. One thing I have noticed that wealthy people share is this: they are surrounded by a lot of green. In their living rooms the abundance of green is striking. You might see, for example, a green sofa, a green carpet, a green painting, or green objects—even their clothes might be green. In other words, the color green is all around them. On the other hand, people who lack money rarely have any green around them. Very often they hate the color. Instead, they surround themselves with depressing colors.

All true Kabbalists know that anyone who understands the use of the color green can be extremely prosperous. Why? The true color of the Sun is green. The Sun is the fountain of life in our Universe. It is the mathematical center of our world. Without the Sun, there is no life. Take a prism and filter the light of the Sun and you will see the seven colors of the spectrum in the order of red, orange, yellow, green, blue, purple and violet. These colors correspond to the seven chakras, or nerve centers, along the spine. The nerve centers are the reflection of the seven great positive centers of consciousness located in the brain. Those seven nerves work through the center of the spine like the seven Archangels before the throne work through the planetary bodies.

The middle color of the spectrum is green, the color of the heart chakra. The heart center, which is nothing less than the reflection of the Sun in us, is also the center of the fulfillment of true desire. Colors are powerful forces that can be used to completely transform our environment. Therefore, when you start to appreciate, contemplate and work with the color green, you can attract opportunities for material and spiritual abundance.

To that effect, yogis who understand the power of sound vibrate certain mantras in order to attract green energy. Those mantras work because of the eighty-four energy points located on the roof of the mouth. These points act as doors to the spiritual world. When the tongue hits certain precise energy points, this in turn changes the molecular frequency of the brain, and attracts blessings that the particular mantra provides. Yogi Bhajan once explained the following mantra to me. Since that time, I have used it with a lot of success. The mantra is:

Har Haray Haree, Wa-he(y) Guru

Har, Harey, Haree is the creative aspect of the infinite manifest in the finite. *Wa-he Guru* is indescribable wisdom. *Guru* is anything that brings you from darkness to light. There are six beats to this mantra. Each of the six beats corresponds to the six directions in space:

Har	*East*
Haray	*North*
Haree	*West*
Wa	*South*
Hey	*Earth or depth*
Guru	*Akasha or height*

MEDITATION FOR GREEN ENERGY AND PROSPERITY: HAR HARAY HAREE

POSITION

1. Sit in easy pose with a straight spine.
2. First clasp the hands together, fingers intertwined at the level of the heart. Then straighten only the index fingers, so they touch and point upwards.
3. The eyes are closed, gently focused at the point between the brows.

MANTRA

Inhale deeply through the nose and exhale completely as you chant:

Har—Haray—Haree—Wa—Hey—Guru

You are at the center. As you vibrate each beat of this sacred mantra, visualize a beautiful field of light, respectively, to the front (HAR), left (HARAY), back (HAREE), right (WA), below (HEY), above (GURU). If you have difficulties visualizing this box-like shape of light, just focus on the mantra; the results will still be positive.

END

Inhale deeply, hold, stretch and exhale. Repeat two more times.

COMMENTS

If you do this everyday for 11 minutes, it will remove deficiency and inefficiency from your life.

A recording of this mantra can be found on the *Greenhouse* CD. See back of book for more information.

Chapter Eight

The Seven Creative Planets

The seven creative planets are the root of practical Kabbalah. They point out with absolute precision the direction in which the forces of Nature are moving, not only for us personally, but also for the entire Universe.

All life responds to a cycle of seven. The entire composition of the body undergoes a change every seven years. There are seven steps in the prenatal existence from the moment of conception to the birth of the child. Seven is called the _Heptad_. It represents the seven major colors and the seven sacraments. It is the number of divine power. Pythagoras considered it a perfect number. Seven signifies the highest attainment of a human on Earth. It is magnetic and favorable by itself. The Pythagoreans called the number 7 the vehiculum of human life. Seven is the number of the soul (3) joined to the body (4). In alchemy, there is what's known as the four elements, and from the compounding results of the three principles or substances are mercury, salt and sulfur. These four elements and three substances symbolize the seven philosophical principles.

The number 7 has played an important role in the history of the world. The 7 races of humanity, the seven wonders of the world, the 7 creative planets and the 7 stars of the Pleiades. There are 7 mystical notes from which all music derives. The Moon passes through 7 days of increase, 7 days full, 7 days of decrease and 7 days of renewal. Four times 7 is twenty-eight in all. There are 7 days of the week, the 7 tones in the human voice, and 7 chords in instrumental music. The lyre has 7 strings. In the womb the child takes 7 distinct formation stages. The body has 7 distinct parts—head, chest, abdomen, two arms, two legs. There are 7 openings in the head—two eyes, two nostrils, two ears and one mouth. These openings in the head correspond to the 7 creative planets. There are 7 internal organs—heart, liver, spleen, two lungs, stomach, two kidneys. For most women, menstruation comes in a series of 4 times 7.

There is a tremendous power in the number seven, and that power is far greater when it manifests itself in nature. Seven influences our destiny, our path in life, and our health. By working with seven we renew our contact with heaven, so that the beneficial heavenly energies may circulate and flow through us and our lives, and we may regain our divine birthright.

The seven creative planets are linked to the cosmic powers of the Archangels. Each of the seven planets is ruled by an Archangel who in turn is subject to God. It is God himself who rules over each of these planets. The person who knows how to work with seven can knowingly attract light and repel darkness.

Everything happens according to time and space. You cannot stop time or change it, but you can alter space to improve your destiny. The secret is in understanding the pattern of creation, and particularly the pattern of seven. God created the world with the 22 letters of the Hebrew alphabet, which relate to the 22 major arcana of the tarot, with the following pattern: three mother letters, seven double letters, and twelve single letters. The letters in this pattern not only correspond to the divine, astral and physical worlds, but they also reveal exactly where our consciousness dwells. For example, the 12 simple letters correspond in space to the 12 signs of the zodiac in astrology. Most of humankind dwells at that level of consciousness. That is why the first thing people often ask you is what astrological sign you are. The fact that seven is the level above twelve, and God uses the pattern of 3–7–12 in the creation of the world, should give us some food for thought.

It may also be interesting to describe here, in as few words as possible, the human spine and its connection to the divine number seven in relation to the pattern of creation. The spinal column is by some mysterious coincidence divided into 26 vertebrae—the exact number of the Kabbalah numerology of the sacred name of God, *Yod He Vav He*, which can only be pronounced with utmost reverence.

Still more extraordinary is the fact that the first section of the spinal column is divided into the seven cervical vertebrae, which corresponds to the seven double letters, the seven creative planets and the seven days of the week. Further, the presence of the mystic number seven in the first group of vertebrae is such a remarkable coincidence that one is forced to the conclusion that the disposition of the sections was purposely planned to come together for a definite reason. And that reason evidently being that the relation of such coincidence will inevitably strike a seeker of truth as an illustration of the power of the number seven as the key to penetrate the mysteries of life and nature. In addition, the seven cervical vertebrae occupying as they do the remarkable position of being the first section, justifies the reason why humans need to work with the number seven, so as to understand and master the laws of nature. This disposition is an epitome of the great truth taught all through the arcanal wisdom.

The other fact is, next to the seven cervical vertebrae, we find the second section of the spine, which is subdivided into twelve thoracic vertebrae and corresponds with the twelve single letters of the Hebrew alphabet, the twelve signs of the zodiac, and the twelve months of the year. Not only is this a curious link to the order of creation, but it is still doubly so, because the seven planets rules the twelve signs of the zodiac. This could only have been done by a supreme and infinite intelligence in order to reveal to us that the mystic number seven, which is at the root of all the laws of nature, is also the key to our health and happiness.

The seven double letters govern the astral world. Each of the seven letters correspond to the seven creative planets, for which the days of the week have been named. This is the central level. Those planets are the Sun, the Moon, Mars, Mercury, Jupiter, Venus and Saturn. The seven Archangels of creation work through them. The twelve signs of the zodiac are ruled by the seven creative planets in the following order: the Sun rules Leo, the Moon rules Cancer, Mars rules Aries and Scorpio, Mercury rules Gemini and Virgo, Jupiter rules Sagittarius and Pisces, Venus rules Taurus and Libra, and Saturn rules Capricorn and Aquarius. Therefore, by operating at the level of the seven creative planets, you control the astral world and everything below, including the physical world and the twelve astrological signs. The astral world is the world of formation. Before anything manifests on the physical plane, it has to go through this world. With an understanding of those planetary energies, you can direct the astral light at will. For he who succeeds in mastering seven knows the principles of all that exists and reaches total fulfillment. Initiates work with the divine number seven in order to read and understand the living language of nature. They show us how to become healthy, happy and holy, and to create a peaceful world where there is no prejudice based on race, color, gender or creed.

After almost three decades of extensive work with universal Kabbalah and yoga, guiding individuals to heal and rise from crossroads, I can honestly say that it is neither enough to practice yoga alone nor is it sufficient to work only with Kabbalah. If you practice yoga and do not spare time to learn the immutable and spiritual laws of nature and know how to apply them, you are short-changing yourself.

I met thousands of yogis from various yoga styles who, had they taken the time to see which way the irresistible forces of nature were moving, could have saved themselves from unnecessary hardship. It was obvious that they could have benefited from Universal Kabbalah. On the other hand, there are Kabbalists who have knowledge of these laws, and yet, they neither know how to breathe nor exercise their physical body. Without question, yoga could have helped strengthen their weak nervous systems and improve their health. In reality, Kabbalists need yoga and yogis can use Universal Kabbalah in the same way the east and west complement each other.

By studying the laws of God and then living in accordance with them, we become free from the suffering and limitation which we have imposed upon our mind, body and spirit. Law and order are heaven's first principle.

The three books *Lifting the Veil*, *Alchemy of Love Relationships*, and *The Splendor of the Sun* reveals these laws. These books, which look deceivingly simple, are not only profound and powerful, but also reveal the microcosmic and macrocosmic formulae, the underlying mystical truth of how humankind can be brought into greater harmony with nature and experience transcendence in physical reality. This will bring divine light forward in mundanity and enable people to reach higher states of consciousness, whereby God may be seen in everybody, every sacred teachings, and in oneself. By reading these principles over and over the Sun of light, truth, and divine wisdom will rise in your heart where it will grow and spread its radiance throughout your whole life. Most importantly, you will find in these books a detailed explanation of the law of the seven creative planets and how they impact every area of our lives. These planets which compose the karmic wheel, are the Universal laws in charge of the regularity and order of everything in heaven and on Earth. They make sure that we fit in with the natural laws, system and order of things to which we owe our being. The laws of the seven creative planets govern our health, life, and love relationships. They are set, and our happiness is linked to our obedience to them, whether we are consciously aware of this or not.

It will not take long for the medical community to discover that the cycle of seven affects diseases and their cure.

Key events at the beginning of life are ordered by these numbers. What happens during the first 7 hours of birth will determine whether a baby will live or not. After the first 7 days the umbilical cord is removed, and 7 days later the baby's eyes begin to be expressive. Seven months later baby teeth begin to appear. Fourteen months later, the baby can stand up and walk securely. After 21 months, the baby can speak (3 sets of 7), and after 28 months, it develops a sense of identity (4 sets of 7). At 35 months (5 sets of 7) comes the weaning period.

This same process can be seen in an adult's life. The first group of 7 years is governed by the Sun. As the Sun acts as manager of this period, the growth of a child is completely assisted by Nature in the first 7 years. The second set of 7 years, between the ages of 7 and 14 are governed by the Moon. The Moon relates to the emotional or inner life, and at this age the child spends much of his or her time in school, learning how to face the realities of life and exploring many new understandings inside himself or herself. It brings puberty.

During the third set of 7 years, Mars rules. It brings manhood/womanhood. This is the period between ages 14 and 21. Mars expresses its influence as strength, war or struggle, and sexual aspects. Naturally, this period's influences are shown in a teen's struggles to build emotional and physical strength and to show secondary sexual characteristics.

Mercury, the planet of communication and intellect, illuminates the period between the ages of 21 to 28. It brings cessation of growth. In this fourth period, the person develops rational thinking, forms concepts and beliefs about the world, and begins to express himself or herself. It brings the prime of strength.

Jupiter, the planet of prosperity and expansion, affects the period between the ages of 28 and 35. During this fifth period, life's opportunities begin to unfold, careers develop and families form.

Venus, the planet of love and fun, rules the period between the ages of 35 and 42. It brings the maturity of mind. During this Venus time, Nature allows us to retain our strength, in order to enjoy the fruits of our labors. This is the sixth period of life.

Saturn rules the period between age 42 and 49. As Saturn's influence relates to discretion and to lessons that develop wisdom, so does the focus of a person's life, during this seventh period before again returning to the Sun. The seventh set of 7 is the highest stage of completion both physically and mentally.

One can observe the impact of the number 7 through these 7 creative planets and cycles. Some Kabbalists follow a different order. They believe the first group of 7 years is ruled by the Moon, the second by Mercury, then Venus, the Sun, Mars, Jupiter and Saturn. I personally hold to the former order.

After the Saturn stage comes the eighth set of 7 where the summit of life is reached. At the ninth set of 7, decline commences. At the tenth set of 7, life become one of weariness. And the cycle continues! As you can see, the number 7 appears continually in our lives, and learning its meaning can lead to greater fulfillment and happiness.

We are all born with intuition. It is our key to happiness. The reality is that people are not always intuitive. Most people use their intuition only twenty percent of the time and live the remaining eighty percent automatically. You cannot be intuitive when your subconscious mind is clouded with garbage. When the subconscious mind is clean, the intuition is clear. If your intuition is not coming through clearly, the pattern of 7 will guide you in your decisions and actions.

The Descending Order of Planets on the Tree of Life

The ancient astrologers took the Earth as the center of our solar system, and provided us with the following order: Neptune, Uranus, Saturn, Jupiter, Mars, the Sun, Venus, Mercury, and the Moon. In fact, this is the order shown in the Tree of Life. Uranus and Neptune, which correspond to the upper trinity of the Tree of Life, only affect the mental aspects of Mother Nature. In that upper trinity, Saturn is the only sphere used in the material plane.

In regard to the order of the planets and the Seal of Solomon: The 7-pointed star or Seal of Solomon, well-known to students of ancient wisdom, shows the pattern of heaven in relation to the planets, as observed in the Temple of Solomon. Following the order of the planets on this sacred seal, we can say that life starts from the

Sun, then goes to the Moon, and proceeds on to Mars, which continues on to Mercury, from Mercury to Jupiter, then to Venus, and from Venus on to Saturn (which symbolizes death), then back to the Sun. This cycle continues endlessly.

THE SEAL OF SOLOMON

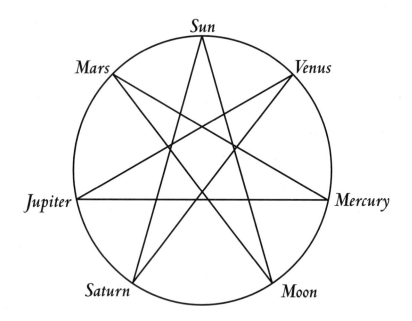

Handwritten marginal note (vertical, left margin): I was born on Venus day and I am a Capricorn (12/25/1992) → My life card is: Death; spiritual transformation!

Practical Application of the Seven Creative Planets

If you do not have a road map and do not know where you are going, it is practically impossible to live a healthy life. The following knowledge is not only helpful in that regard, but it is also of an intensely practical nature. The accuracy of this system has been proved by countless people—including this author, through numerous experiments and experiences. My goal is to make this system so clear that anyone, regardless of his or her intellectual level or background, can apply it to his or her life with success.

The seven days of the week follow the same pattern of the sacred seal. The seven days of creation of the world, mentioned in the book of Genesis, correspond to the seven planets. Those planets are each ruled by one of the seven angels that God has put in charge of heaven and Earth. Those angels use the planets as channels to carry out their responsibilities.

In other words, every human being has a vibration and his or her life has a particular rhythm. Certain segments of the rhythms are ruled by particular forces that we call planets. The names that we give the planets are a way to identify the forces behind these rhythms. Whether we know it or not, human life is strongly influenced by these rhythms. Here is the way to define those rhythms. There are 365 days in a year; divided by seven, one arrives at seven periods of 52 days each. Each period of 52 days is governed by a planet. Your personal yearly cycle proceeds from your birthday to the day before your birthday. Therefore, each of these seven periods starting from your birthday will be respectively governed by the Sun, the Moon, Mars, Mercury, Jupiter, Venus, and Saturn.

The Earth goes through a yearly cycle. The planetary year does not start on January 1, even though this is what our current calendar system states. The new year actually begins on March 21, the first day of Spring. This is the first powerful day of the year, when the Sun releases vast amounts of energy into the Universe. Each individual has a personal yearly cycle as well, with the first day of the Sun period starting on your birthday. For example, if you were born on March 21, which is also the first day of the Earth's year, this is what the seven periods of 52 days would look like for you:

EXAMPLE OF THE YEARLY CYCLE FOR
A PERSON BORN ON MARCH 21

Sun Period:	March 21–May 11
Moon Period:	May 12–July 2
Mars Period:	July 3–August 23
Mercury Period:	August 24–October 14
Jupiter Period:	October 15–December 5
Venus Period:	December 6–January 26
Saturn Period:	January 27–March 20

Our world is one of duality. Therefore, life is governed by the principle of vibration. Vibration is symbolized by up and down, day and night, good and evil, etc. Within your cycle some planets represent our best times and others, our challenging times. For example, the Sun, Jupiter, and Venus are beneficent planets, whereas Mars and Saturn are challenging planets. The Moon and Mercury remain neutral; they can go either way.

You need only experiment with the seven creative planets for a few months, when you will be forced to notice how easily things turn for you during your Sun, Jupiter and Venus periods. You will be struck with the strong fact that under these three beneficial periods, things will be favorable for your plans or business, and you will display much more magnetism during these periods of the year. You will notice too that the same law applies to your own vitality and health. For example, how you have felt "down" at certain periods of the year, which you will notice come regularly when you have not been within the favorable period indicated for you.

If you are open-minded, you will begin to apply this knowledge to all your actions. You will no longer make appointments at random. You will then begin to notice how much easier the machinery of your affairs works, you will no longer lose your head or be frightened when worries appear to come from every side. You can then expect challenges at certain periods and make your plans accordingly. In a short time, you will notice how much more successful you have become and how, with less effort in every sense, more can be accomplished.

You will then begin to apply the same rules to your home. You will no longer be as fearful and anxious when you feel there is nothing to guide you. You will know when to expect those moments of depression and vulnerability when your love relationship is going through challenges. You will no longer seek solace in drugs, smoking, alcohol or bars. God, the great Architect of the Universe and giver of life, regulates everything in our solar system and beyond, including the actions of humans. To the most unsuccessful, this blueprint will bring success. To those who are already successful, it will bring higher opportunities for them to experience their vastness.

On the following pages are descriptions and detailed explanations of the jurisdiction of each of the seven creative planets, their attributes, their corresponding Archangels, and how each pertains to your personal affairs.

*There is nothing more fascinating than
working with the divine spiritual wisdom.
The time and energy spent in working with this
sacred science will be repaid seven-hundred fold.*

—Joseph Michael Levry (Gurunam)

SUN

The Sun period is your first planetary period. It is a time of great growth and strength. This potent Sun period begins the day of your birthday and, as with all periods, lasts for 52 days. The Sun period is an excellent time to engage with superiors, employers, executives and officials. This is the time to speak with your boss about work-related problems and work on business deals and plans.

Imagination is another hallmark of your Sun period. The Sun period is a time of rebirth because the planetary cycle is beginning anew. You will feel alive and inspired, illuminated by the Sun's great strength and inspired by its optimism. Mental powers are acute at this time. You will feel ready for anything and afraid of no one.

All that pertains to health matters is a featured characteristic of the Sun period. Maintaining health through diet and exercise and attaining your health-related goals are entirely within reach during your Sun period. Because the Sun is a projection of Jupiter, it rules the general medical field and the lower courts.

This is a period when the Universe gives you the green light to do and be anything you want. It provides you with an abundance of new energy. This is a time for growth and expansion. You can start or accomplish anything you want, and many opportunities will come to you. This is your lucky time—you can borrow or invest money, ask for a raise or favor, and improve your reputation. You can get a new pet. All the obstacles that may have prevented you from having what you want will easily be overcome.

This is the time to put your productive ideas into practical form. Use determination and strength to welcome new ideas, new activities, new experiences and new acquaintances. This is a favorable time to seek advancement in social and business ventures, further your ambitions, seek a new job, make new friend, embark on a journey. This is the time to assert yourself, exercise your initiative and demonstrate your leadership.

In a few rare cases, for seven days your Sun period may be overlapped by the cusp of the previous period, Saturn. In some cases, it may not come into full strength until or about seven days after your birthday. Sometimes, for seven days before your Sun period ends, it gradually loses it's strength on account of becoming overlapped by the cusp of the incoming Moon period.

ARCHANGEL: Raphael
Healing of God—gives health and wealth

MOON

The next 52 days encompasses your Moon period. The Moon emphasizes dealings with the general public, women and feminine principles, and fluctuation. Aspects of your personality, removal, cleansing, changes, and short journeys are all especially influenced by the Moon in this period. The Moon rules the general medical field, the home, housekeeping, cooking, babies and small children. During your Moon period do not let disharmony and disagreeable situations take a toll on your nervous system. Diplomacy is the order of the day. Affairs may progress slowly. Your Moon period is the time to cooperate with others and keep your temper at an even level. You should be diplomatic and avoid arguments. In other words, be cool. This is a time to work with others, observe, listen. Minor changes will take place in your routine—you may feel that you are vacillating and unable to make up your mind about vital issues. If you find it difficult to make up your mind, wait for the next period. Develop discipline and a definite purpose and speak with moderation and forethought.

Natural scientists, ancient wise men, and spiritual scholars have always known that the Moon has a significant influence upon plant life, animal life, and upon psychic activities in human beings. Most students of nature know that animals, birds and reptiles are more active on the full Moon, and that their reproductive cycles and basic life movements are influenced by the Moon's alterations. There is also an absolute correspondence between human feminine functions and the twenty-eight day lunar cycle.

Everyone is influenced by the Moon, but during our Moon period we are doubly influenced. The Moon's waxing and waning is very significant. Positive Earth pulsations are manifested in increased light from the new Moon to the full Moon lasting about 14-15 days. The negative pulsations are shown in the Moon's decrease from the full Moon to the new Moon. Remember, the time during the waxing Moon is an excellent time to add elements to your life. Time during the waning Moon is an excellent time to remove elements from your life.

If you start a project, it should be completed within this period. Do not start a new job. Realize that if you do, the change will not be long-term. This is the best time for short trips. It is a good time to deal with the public. Men will get along better with women than with other men. The Moon period is also a good time for marriage proposals.

ARCHANGEL: Gabriel
Power of God—gives peace and harmony

MARS

The next 52 days will take you through the Mars period. Although this is most often a challenging period, there are some exciting aspects to this period as well. Will power, magnetism, vitality of the body, and sexual energy are increased during this period. There is a headstrong quality to every aspect of life during your Mars period and while sometimes this is beneficial, other times it is a great hindrance. War, anger, and haste are characteristics of the Mars period. Construction/destruction, the work of dentists and surgeons, and athletes benefits during their Mars period.

During this period, the Universe will put a lot of energy at your disposal, either to improve your health or to do anything of a physical nature. You will have an abundance of physical energy. Therefore, this is the best time to exercise and work out. Use this energy to remove obstacles that may have prevented you from moving forward. Use critical judgment in this time. Feel empowered and be the one who makes the rules. You may be tempted to do projects that will not benefit you. For women, it is the best period in which to ask men for anything. Mars is a planet of trials and tests. This challenging planet stands for guns, fire, accidents and sexuality. Exercise caution during this time. Your Mars period is not a good time for initiating anything of importance. Do not enter into any legally binding situations that may be unclear.

Mars reveals its combative qualities even in our own bodies. It influences both the muscular system and the immune system, plus the bone marrow, which manufactures white blood corpuscles to fight off viruses and bacteria. It has a direct relationship to the blood and is closely related to the muscular system. Mars rules over courage which is directly related to blood sugar levels.

Mars may influence you to make rash decisions. Learn to be patient. Be careful of what you say and write. Examine carefully any agreement or other documents requiring your signature. Do not waste any of your forces on complaining or activities which bring no positive results.

Use the great forces at your disposal in this period to push through obstacles to your positive plans. This is a good time to cast off the useless and prepare to begin anew. All that requires force and strong, prompt action, such as contests, sports, games, hunting, fighting, wrestling, public agitation and movements, will benefit from Mars.

Mars can cause one to be short-tempered, argumentative, rest-less, unstable, and cruel. Because Mars has a destabilizing influence, it makes people prone to illegal ventures and illicit love affairs. Do not allow Mars to tempt you into compromising any love relationships and your self respect.

ARCHANGEL: Kamael
Desire of God—gives divine protection from all aggression

MERCURY

The next 52 days welcome the Mercury period. Communication and writing are highlights of the Mercury period. Business matters, authors and their writing, and written contracts will all benefit under Mercury's influence. Mental judgments are acute during Mercury. Travel and buying and selling in business are favored. Learning is enhanced, therefore assimilating and disseminating knowledge will seem easier during this intellectual and communicative planet's period. All that is written on paper, books, magazines, newspapers, etc., may play a special part.

You may experience a lot of changes during this period. Sometimes you may feel as if you are in a battlefield, where the only thing you have for guidance is your intuition. Your intuitive intelligence should be used to the utmost during this time, when mental and spiritual bodies are stimulated. It is the best time to put your ideas to work, write books, study, collect information and make plans. This is the best time to deal with children. Go with the flow, but be very discriminating. Do not leave your personal belongings unattended.

Advertise your wares and seek favorable publicity. Accept any change with open arms. Keep in communication with people who are far away, as this may lead to an unexpected opportunity. Exercise your judgment and discrimination, for deceit is in the air and you may be taken in. Activities that will be fruitful: starting to write a new book or musical composition, writing letters and all forms of communication, registering for a course of study, selling subscriptions, reasoning with children, making new acquaintances, making a public debut, business shopping and bargain hunting. Editors, those who work with analysis and statistics, and intellectuals will be greatly influenced. This is an excellent time to be optimistic and try to express yourself orally and through writing.

ARCHANGEL: Michael
Who is like God—gives success and intelligence

JUPITER

Jupiter has its say for the next 52 days. Jupiter rules the general medical realm and regulates financial matters and wealth. Jupiter stands for business and trading of all kinds, investments, banking and dealing with the bank officials, religious ceremonial functions, seeking favors, settlements in litigation, ceremonial and philanthropic occasions of every kind to help others and incidentally help oneself.

Jupiter is the planet of material and spiritual abundance. This is the time when the lord of prosperity will easily smile upon you. Take this time to prosper and expand. Be ambitious and take risks, such as buying stocks. During this period, resolve matters of the law. Jupiter rules the higher courts. It is a good time to deal with lawyers, judges, government officials and people of wealth. You may easily gain popularity in this period. This is a good time to take a chance and some calculated risks. Speculation, gambling and the stock exchange are areas where success might be easier to come by now. Obtaining personal favors of financial nature, dealings with bankers, creditors, and debtors are almost sure to occur. All types of improvement, abundance, growth and expansion infuse these 52 days in Jupiter's reign.

This is a time to use determination to fulfill every one of your potentialities. Your mental outlook will be of major importance here. Cosmic forces are working with you, so promote your favorite ambition. Fruitful activities: attending to legal matters, consulting people in positions of authority with tact, dealing with charitable institutions, seeking election to any office, attending to matters of employment, visiting loved ones.

ARCHANGEL: Tsadkiel
Justice of God—brings good fortune

VENUS

The next 52 days belong to Venus. Venus rules art and artists and has a hand in the performing arts, music, theater, and opera. All beauty and pleasure, extravagance, luxury, and self-indulgence will find a way to delight you during your Venus period. Parties and social affairs will fill your calendar now and you will find new ways to enjoy your life. Perfume and sweet scents, aphrodisiacs, love affairs and romance will renew your passion for living.

Loosen up. The Venus period is time for rest, play, and fun. It is an excellent time to get involved with music, art and dance. You should now take good care of yourself and treat yourself right.

Surround yourself with beauty and harmony. This is a time for beauty, art, desire and culture. Try to enhance the beauty of your surroundings, for the vibrations are favorable for the increase of enjoyment through the decorative arts. Fruitful activities: entering a partnership, taking beauty treatments. It is the best time for taking long or short trips, improving relationships and making friends. Men can ask women for anything. This is an excellent time to concern yourself with a new partner, rekindle a romance with a tried and true love, propose marriage, and marry.

ARCHANGEL: Hanael
Grace of God—bestows love and happiness

SATURN

Saturn is a well-known challenging planet. The next 52 days will require precise attention to detail and emotional balance. Debts and their repayment will be highlighted. This time is conducive to deep study, concentration, exact and just reasoning. Aspects of life having to do with the Earth and longevity are important to Saturn. Dealing in property and real estate, farming and gardening, mortgages and the elderly will be at the forefront of this period. Death wills, inheritances, old buildings, trees, landlords and land owners may make an appearance. Inertia may accompany every action and decision.

This is a time requiring an absolute balanced and unemotional state of mind. Let your meditations and analysis lead you to the discovery of truths both ancient and new, especially along spiritual lines of thought. You may feel confined or restricted. This is a time to study yourself, your friends and your environment with a detachment that is cool and clear. Be grateful for this chance to see things as they are. Be prepared to cast off the impediments of life that are not working for you or worth your while. Saturn, who is the balancer of karma, is also referred to as the planet of darkness. It brings disturbance in the mind, body and spirit, making you lonely and frustrated. It is confining and limiting. Saturn reveals in a hard way what is not working in your life and where you need to change. It can bring humiliation, delays, obstacles, and problems with the law. Take this time to rest and regroup; meditate and further your spiritual development. Your Saturn period is one of the worst times for initiating anything of importance; do not sign any legal contracts. You may be tempted to take foolish actions and make poor decisions. This is the best time to exercise discipline. Avoid scandal and gossip. You may feel restricted in this period or feel that everything is proceeding slowly. Check up on your health; you are most susceptible to health and skin diseases at this time. Use this period to look within and study both yourself and your surroundings. Do not miss meditation, and do not let a day go by without strengthening your aura. Get rid of anything you do not need. Try to study and understand the unseen forces that direct our lives. Spend a lot of time reading inspirational books, such as the Bible, the Koran, the Siri Guru Granth Sahib, the Zohar, etc.

Although Saturn is challenging in many respects, it is a good time to deal with real estate matters. Therefore, consider the purchase of property or beginning spiritual studies. Most important, Withdraw! Every soul needs to withdraw from the world from time to time to find the peace which is beyond understanding. At this time in your planetary cycle, you deserve to renew your energy source. Once you can establish that peace, you can go anywhere and do anything without confusion and chaos affecting you in any way. Times of peace and stillness are very precious in a world of constant stimulation and change.

ARCHANGEL: Tsaphkiel

Contemplation of God—bestows blessings of knowledge and understanding

Working with the Seven Periods and the Phases of the Moon

Important note on Mars and Saturn: You can still do many things during your Mars and Saturn periods. This is not a cut and dry system where you must be frozen and not do anything during these times. This system is designed to make you aware of how these unseen forces influence your life. I have personally found that keeping a consistent prayer practice, especially doing the mantras in the morning from *Triple Mantra, Heaven's Touch, Lumen de Lumine, RaMaDaSa,* or *Green House* help make things flow. *(See end of book for more information on these CDs.)*

CASE A:

Say you are in your Sun period and you decide either to get married during this time or to start a new business. From the foregoing, you know that the Sun, Jupiter and Venus are positive periods. Therefore, you will find yourself in a very favorable position. When the Moon is waxing, the positive effects are greater than during the waning Moon. So if you have a choice, the most logical thing to do is take action on the waxing Moon during this period.

✓ CASE B:

Suppose you are in your Saturn period. You now know that Mars and Saturn are challenging periods. Therefore, they are even more challenging during the waning Moon. If you were to initiate something new in this time, it would be preferable to wait for the waxing Moon, because you will find this time to be less challenging than when the Moon is waning.

CASE C:

The Mercury and Moon periods follow the fluctuations of the Moon. In other words, the waxing Moon renders Mercury and Moon periods favorable. The waning Moon, being negative, makes initiating projects more challenging.

Historical Examples

A person who does not know what to do is at mercy of whatever life throws his or her way. Let's take as an example the well-known case of President Clinton and Monica Lewinsky to demonstrate the accuracy of this system. President Clinton met Monica Lewinsky within 52 days before his birthday, while he was in his *Saturn* period. Through his weaknesses, Saturn caused Monica to become a near-fatal blow to his destiny. The court papers with Paula Jones were signed in January during his *Mars* period. Another blow to his career. August 17 was the worst possible day for Clinton to make his confession on national TV, because as mentioned above, that date fell within his Saturn period. In addition, August is the 8th month of the year and 8 stands for Saturn. When the day is reduced (17=1+7) the result is 8. This day had a triple-Saturn impact on Clinton. Saturn, who is the balancer of karma, is also referred to as the planet of darkness. It brings disturbance to the mind, body and spirit, making you lonely and frustrated. It is confining and limiting. Saturn reveals in a hard way what is not working in your life and where you need to change. It can bring humiliation, delays, obstacles, and problems with the law, such as lawsuits. The Congressional decision to proceed with the impeachment hearing took place on October 8—two days before the end of Clinton's *Sun* period. The Sun rules the first 52 days after your birthday. It is a very favorable time for improving your reputation and shining light on all your affairs. Therefore, the Sun was a major factor in elevating Clinton's reputation during this trying time.

ADDITIONAL EXAMPLES

Parnell, the great Irish leader, was married during his *Saturn* period. This led to a divorce causing his political downfall.

George Washington, born April 30, 1789, was elected President of the United States during his *Sun* period in the month of May. Interestingly, Washington and twelve of his generals were Freemasons.

Abraham Lincoln, born February 12, 1809, was inaugurated into office as the President of the United States during his *Sun* period

Franklin D. Roosevelt was born on January 30, 1882, and took office as assistant of the navy on March 17, during his *Sun* period.

Stalin and Lenin came into power during their *Sun* periods.

Napoleon Bonaparte was born on August 15. He joined the Republican Army of France during his *Sun* period—September 16, 1703, which led to his fame. On June 29, 1815, during his *Saturn* period, he boarded a British warship, which eventually led to his exile and humiliation.

Hitler was born on April 20. He decided to invade Norway on March 1 during his *Saturn* period. It was a disaster. He lost 30 ships, five cruisers and seven destroyers at Narvick.

Italy became a nation in July. Mussolini, who was born on July 29, declared war on both France and Britain on June 10, while he and his country were both in their *Saturn* period. It was a disaster.

Germany became an empire on January 1, 1871. She surrendered to her enemies on November 11, 1918 during her *Saturn* period.

This system is designed as a guide to allow you to see the unseen forces which control our lives, so that you may use your free will constructively. In the words of one Rose+Croix, "Do not be slave to any system of analysis." *The God of your Heart should be your ultimate guide.*

Chapter Nine

Meditations for the Seven Periods

The following meditations were originally taught by Yogi Bhajan, master of Kundalini yoga and White Tantric yoga. I have presented them here in such a manner that will be most beneficial for each particular period, in deflecting negative influences and bringing out the positive aspects of the planetary energy. When you are in a particular period, choose one meditation that feels right for you and work with it throughout the 52 days. Be consistent, but *please* don't overdo it by practicing all the meditations.

It is very important to begin your meditation or Kundalini yoga practice by tuning in before you begin. It is also recommended to tune out at the end to consolidate and integrate your energies. Use the Adi Mantra (**Ong Namo Guru Dev Namo**) to tune in and the Bij Mantra (**Sat Nam**) to tune out.

ADI MANTRA

You can quickly center yourself through a few repetitions of the Adi Mantra. It opens the protective channel for energy to flow and tunes you into the Supreme Consciousness. From practical experience, it is suggested that you tune in with this before starting all meditations and exercises. Breath gives power to the mantra, so always chant after taking a full breath through the nose.

Audio cassettes or CD recordings of some of the following mantras may be obtained through: *Rootlight, Inc.* 212-769-8115 www.rootlight.com; *Golden Temple Enterprises* 800-829-3970; *Cherdi Kala Music* 310-550-6893 www.cherdikala.com; *Ancient Healing Ways* 800-359-2940 www.a-healing.com.

1. Sit either in Easy Pose with the legs crossed or in a chair, with the feet flat on the floor, spine straight.
2. Press your palms together in prayer pose, thumbs at the sternum. Close the eyes.
3. Chant at least three times. Do the first part on one breath (ONG NAMO), take another breath and do the second part (GURU DEV NAMO). Feel the sound resonating through your head.

Ong Namo,
Guru Dev Namo

This means *I call on the infinite creative consciousness. I call on the divine within.* By chanting this mantra, you will be establishing a protective link in the chain of golden light from you to your teacher, who is in turn, linked to his teacher and to the Divine Source. This mantra, when chanted in proper consciousness, opens the connection between the self and the divine teacher within. Therefore, you are calling on your higher Self and all other beings of light for guidance and protection.

BIJ MANTRA

Sat Nam is the Bij Mantra, which means "the name of God is truth," "true identity," and "Truth is my identity." This is a universal mantra whose sound embodies truth itself. It is used to connect with the infinity that is within you. Use this mantra to exit from your meditations.

1. Place your hands in prayer pose.
2. Inhale deeply. On the exhale, chant a long SAT and a short NAM.

Saaaaaaat Nam

SUN PERIOD

Meditations to bring out the beneficial aspects of the Sun

❋

Sodarchan Chakra Kriya

❋

Kriya: Sadhana Yojina

❋

Meditation for Human Quality

❋

Meditation for Synchronicity and Protection

❋

Inner Sun: Immune System Booster

SODARCHAN CHAKRA KRIYA

Here is a meditation that makes use of prana to cleanse mental garbage and purify the mind. It is an excellent meditation to do in your Sun period and also during the season of Spring.

Of all the 20 types of yoga, including Kundalini yoga, this is the highest kriya. This is a very powerful meditation for prosperity. It will give you a new start. It is the simplest kriya, but at the same time the hardest. It cuts through all darkness and all barriers of a neurotic or psychotic nature. When a person is in a very bad state, techniques imposed from the outside will not work. The pressure has to be stimulated from within.

The tragedy of life occurs when the subconscious releases garbage into the conscious mind. This kriya invokes the Kundalini to give you the necessary vitality and intuition to combat the negative effects of the subconscious mind.

POSITION

Sit with spine straight (either on the floor with legs crossed, or sit in a chair with feet flat on the floor). The eyes are focused at the tip of the nose, or closed if you prefer.

MUDRA AND BREATH

1. Block off the right nostril with the right thumb. Inhale slowly and deeply through the left nostril and hold the breath. Mentally chant WA-HE GURU 16 times, while pumping the navel point 3 times with each repetition (pump once on WAA, once on HEY and once on GURU), for a total of 48 pumps. WA is infinity; HE is the presence of the finite in infinity; GU is darkness; and RU is light. Together WA-HE GURU means *Indescribable Wisdom.*

2. Unblock the right nostril and use the right index or pinkie finger to block the left nostril. Exhale slowly and deeply through the right nostril. Continue, inhaling left nostril, exhaling right.

To end the meditation, inhale and hold 5–10 seconds. Exhale. Then stretch and shake the body for about 1 minute to circulate the energy.

TIME
Suggested length for this kriya is 31 or 62 minutes a day. The ideal is to start at 31 minutes, but you can begin with 11 minutes, then build up to 31, then 40, and eventually 62.

COMMENTS
There is no time, no place, no space, and no condition attached to this meditation. Each garbage pit has its own time to clear. If you are going to clean your own garbage, you must estimate and clean it as fast as you can, or as slowly as you want. You have to decide how much time you have to clean up your garbage pit. If you can do this meditation for 62 minutes to start with, then build up to the point where you can do it 2 1/2 hours a day (1/10th of the day), it will give you *Nao nidhi, athara sidhi*, which are the 9 precious virtues and 18 occult powers. In these 27 total virtues of the world lies the entire Universe.

Practiced 2 1/2 hours every day, this meditation will make you a perfect superhuman. It will purify the subconscious and take care of your life. It will make you extremely intuitive. It brings together all 27 facets of life and makes people saintly, successful and qualified. This meditation also gives you pranic power. This kriya never fails. It can give you inner happiness and bring you to a state of ecstasy in life.

KRIYA: SADHANA YOJINA

This meditation can wipe out every weakness in your destiny, your surroundings and your connections.

POSITION

Sit with a straight spine, with the legs crossed in easy pose, or sit in a chair with the weight of both feet equally distributed on the ground. The eyes are $1/10$th open.

HANDS

Interlock the fingers of the hands together with the palms facing down. Firmly press the thumbs together and force them as far under the palms as possible. Hold the hand position in front of the body at the level of the throat. Keep the thumbs firmly pressed together and locked under the palms. You may experience some pain but do not give an inch. Elbows are parallel to the ground.

BREATH

Breathe only when necessary, and in quick breaths in order to maintain the continuous rhythm of the mantra.

MANTRA

Be sure to keep the vocal pitch at a constant level throughout the meditation. Chant in a continuous, unbroken rhythm and monotone voice:

Gobinday Mukanday Udaray Aparay
Haring Karing Nirnamay Akamay

This mantra means: *Sustainer, Liberator, Enlightener, Infinite, Destroyer, Creator, Nameless, Desireless.*

LOCKS OR OTHER FOCUS

Focus on the breath and the mantra.

TIME: 11–30 minutes per day for 90 days.

MEDITATION FOR HUMAN QUALITY

This meditation opens the power of the fourth chakra. It balances and repairs the sympathetic nervous system. It helps the physical heart. It gives resistance to tension and high pressure environments. The greatest result is that it connects you with the inner sense of being human.

POSITION

Sit in an easy cross-legged pose, keeping the spine straight. Place both hands in the form of Ravi mudra: Touch the tip of the ring finger to the tip of the thumb. Extend both arms parallel to the ground with the palms down. Spread the fingers wide. Put the sides of the tips of the index fingers together. Raise the arms slightly so the index fingernails are at the level of the eyes. Keep the eyes relaxed and open. Look over the index fingertips to the horizon. Just hold this position completely still.

Continue for a *maximum* of 11 minutes.

COMMENTS

We often fail in life and in our capacity for devotion because we are not trained to use our human qualities. These qualities of endurance, creativity and compassion are regulated by the third, fourth and fifth chakras. The first and second chakras are below human. The sixth, seventh and eighth chakras are beyond human. So it is only in the area of the heart that we can fulfill our nature.

Meditation for Synchronicity and Protection

POSITION

Sit in Easy Pose with the legs crossed or in any meditative sitting posture with a straight spine. Relax the arms down with the elbows bent. Interlace the fingers of both hands and press the palms together, pointing away from the body. Press the right side of the left thumb against the left side of the right thumb and rest the joined thumbs on the index finger which is immediately beneath them. Now raise the forearms up until the hands are in front of the chest at the level of the heart.

EYES

The eyes are $^1/_{10}$th open.

BREATH

Deeply inhale and completely exhale as the mantra is chanted.

MANTRA

Chant the following mantra 5 times in a monotone voice as the breath is completely exhaled. This repetition takes about fifteen seconds. You may find it very helpful to chant along with the CD recording *Heaven's Touch*, track 1. (See the back of the book for information where to obtain this recording.)

Guru Guru Waa-hey Guru
Guru Raam Daas Guru

TIME

Meditate for 11–31 minutes. This can be practiced at any time.

COMMENTS

This meditation will totally neutralize the energy flow within the body and build a tremendous protective aura. It brings the mind, body and spirit into a state of harmony, and enables you to meditate on your own divine force, your own fiber. For a detailed description of this mantra, refer to page 221.

MEANING OF MANTRA

Guru Guru Wahe Guru, Guru Ram Das Guru
The wisdom that comes as a servant of the infinite

INNER SUN: IMMUNE SYSTEM BOOSTER

This meditation works on cleansing and rejuvenating your whole system. The immune system will have new vigor and will not be blocked by inner conflict.

POSITION

Sit in Easy Pose with a straight spine. Close your eyes and concentrate at the brow point. *Left hand:* bend your elbow and raise your hand to shoulder level, as if taking an oath. Touch the tip of the ring, or Sun, finger to the tip of the thumb, called Surya Mudra. *Right hand:* make a fist, then extend the index finger and use it to close off the right nostril.

BREATH

Begin a steady and powerful Breath of Fire—a rapid equal inhale and exhale from the diaphragm—through the left nostril.

TIME: Start with 3 minutes, then gradually work up to 31. To end, inhale deeply and hold the breath. As you hold, interlace the fingers of the hands 4 inches away from the face, palms facing towards you. Try to pull the fingers apart using resistance and creating a great tension. When you must, exhale. Repeat 3 more times. Relax.

COMMENTS

This breath meditation strengthens the immune system by allowing us to access the healing and nurturing energy from the Moon, mother of life, in order to renew the blood, help the nervous system, and take care of the glandular system. Our fears, insecurities, shame, anger, frustration, and guilt are destructive and unhealthy emotions that lead to depression. They prevent the immune system from working properly. This lunar breath heals the emotional body by helping to clear out these unhealthy energies. During this meditation, you may go through emotional shifts while your body is regaining balance. Then you will begin to experience the calm, peacefulness and harmony that comes with healing impact.

MOON PERIOD

Meditations to bring out the beneficial aspects of the Moon

❋

Ganpati Kriya

❋

Moon Kriya

❋

Meditation to Remove Fear and Obstacles

❋

Meditation to Totally Recharge You

GANPATI KRIYA

Our five fingers correspond to the five *tattvas* (elements) of which everything in this Universe is made. Prana is the expression of the five elements in harmonious action.

The palms are the face of one's astral body. The astral body is between the mental and physical bodies. Therefore, anything that is to happen on the material plane must first go through the astral plane. A person can change his or her destiny by first creating change on the astral level.

Pressing the thumb to each fingertip applies the science through which each can rewrite his or her destiny. It balances the five elements, thereby bringing the mind, body, emotions, and spirit into harmony.

Ganpati Kriya (pronounced gun-puti) is a very sacred kriya. Ganpati means *Ganesha*, the elephant God who rode on the back of a rat that could go anywhere. It is also called the impossible-possible kriya, whereby all negativity from the past and present will be redeemed. Ganpati is sometimes called *Mangalam*, the God of happiness.

This meditation deals with samskaras, karma, and dharam. It will take away all *samskaras*, all the negative karmas that you carry from past lives and have to pay for now. The sufferings we have are only because of past debt and past credit.

It also takes away the karma you create from what you do in your day-to-day life. It creates the way for dharam, the good you do today that will be rewarded tomorrow.

MUDRA

Sit in Easy Pose, spine straight, elbows straight, wrists resting on your knees. You will be pressing your thumb to alternating fingers with each sound. Keep your eyes closed. Chant in an even rhythm to this simple tune for 11 minutes:

Sa - Ta - Na - Ma   Ra - Ma - Da - Sa   Sa - Say - So - Hung

a. SA: Press the thumb to the index finger. *(Jupiter/Water element)*
b. TA: Press the thumb to the middle finger. *(Saturn/Fire element)*
c. NA: Press the thumb to the ring finger. *(Sun/Air element)*
d. MA: Press the thumb to the baby finger. *(Mercury/Ether element)*
Continue finger pattern through
RA-MA-DA-SA
SA-SAY-SO-HUNG

END

Inhale deeply, then move and rotate your body as if going through physical spasms. Every muscle must be stretched, squeezed, and moved, from the muscles in your face, head and neck, down to your toes. The idea is to circulate the prana to every part of your body. The breath is held approximately 35 seconds. Repeat this procedure, with the breath held in, at total of 4 times. Finally, inhale, sit calmly and concentrate on the tip of your nose for 20 seconds. Then relax.

MEANING OF MANTRA

Sa–Ta–Na–Ma	*Existence–Life–Death–Rebirth*
Ra–Ma–Da–Sa	*Sun–Moon–Earth–Infinity*
Sa–Say–So–Hung	*Infinity–I am thou*

MOON KRIYA

MUDRA

Sitting in Easy Pose with a straight spine, touch the elbows to waist, while extending the forearms out in front, so they are parallel to the ground, palms facing up. Make the palms into loose fists, with the thumbs on the outside and pinkies on the inside.

MOVEMENT

1. Bring the sides of the hands together, hitting the fleshy area of the hands below the pinkie finger together very forcefully. This is the area of the hand known as the moon center. Chant **Har** as you strike.

2. Move the hands apart, separating them by 12 inches (fists will separate until they are above the knees) and flip the wrists until they are palm down. Continue this movement in a steady motion.

MANTRA

Chant **Har, Har, Har,** continuously in a monotone, by striking the tongue against the upper palate each time you chant the word. Pull the navel slightly with each recitation. Every time you chant one *Har,* you will also strike the hands together at the same time. The meaning of *Har* is *the creative aspect of infinity.*

MUSIC
A rhythmic drum tape

TIME
Practice for 9 minutes.

END
Inhale deeply and hold 6–10 seconds as you hit the Moon centers together forcefully. Exhale. Repeat 3 times.

COMMENTS/EFFECTS
When the Moon centers hit, navel pulls in and the tip of the tongue strikes the upper palate, it has the effect of bringing clarity and realism. People are always striving to be energetic and neglecting to eliminate fatigue. It is important to live *sattvic*—in a state of purity, which allows you to be calm and cool. *Sattvic* is life without fatigue and tension. You always feel that you are great when you are very energetic. Actually, you are great when you are sober, calm and living in your sustained saintly self.

Meditation to Remove Fear and Obstacles

This meditation directs your fear toward motivating you to infinity. "It will bring a simple polarity of your own magnetic field and anything which has been neutralized and is weak with you, it will make you strong."

POSITION

Sit with the legs crossed or in a chair with the weight of both feet equally distributed on the ground. Bend the neck and lock the chin down against the chest.

ARMS AND HANDS

Relax the arms down with the elbows bent. Raise the forearms up and in toward the chest, until the hands meet in front of the chest at the level of the heart. Extend and join all fingers and the thumb of each hand and place the right hand immediately above the left hand. Point the palm of the left hand down at the ground and the palm of the right hand up at the sky. The hands should be parallel to each other and to the ground. This is easiest done by keeping the forearms parallel to the ground.

BREATH

Begin the meditation by deeply inhaling and completely exhaling 3 times. Then deeply inhale and completely exhale as the mantra is chanted. Upon completion of the meditation, deeply inhale, hold the breath for an extended period of time and completely exhale. Repeat the breathing process 2 more times.

EYES

Look at the tip of the nose.

MANTRA

Chant the complete mantra on the exhale. Pull in the navel on the *Such*.

> *Ad Such, Jugad Such, Haibee Such, Nanaka Hosee Bee Such*
> *Ad Such, Jugad Such, Haibee Such, Nanaka Hosee Bee Such*
> *Ad Such, Jugad Such, Haibee Such, Nanaka Hosee Bee Such*

TIME

Begin with 11 minutes and slowly build the time to 31 minutes.

MEANING OF MANTRA

The literal translation of this mantra is
It is true in the beginning,
true through the ages,
and true even now.
Nanak shall ever be true.

MEDITATION TO TOTALLY RECHARGE YOU

This meditation totally recharges you. It is an antidote to depression. It builds a new system, gives you the capacity and caliber to deal with life, and gives you a direct relationship with your pranic body.

POSITION

Sit with a straight spine in Easy Pose.

MUDRA

Arms are extended straight out in front of you, parallel to the ground. Close your right hand into a fist. Wrap your left fingers around it. The base of the palms touch. The thumbs are close together and are pulled straight up. The eyes are focused on the thumbs.

Now inhale for 5 seconds (do not hold the breath in); exhale for 5 seconds; hold the breath out for 15 seconds. Continue.

TIME

Start with 3–5 minutes and work up to 11 minutes. Build up the time slowly. In time, you can work up to holding the breath out for 1 full minute.

MARS PERIOD

Meditations to bring out the beneficial aspects of Mars

❀

Brahm Mudra Meditation

❀

Meditation to Melt Negativity

❀

For When You Don't Know What to Do

❀

When Nothing Else Works

BRAHM MUDRA MEDITATION

This mudra changes the metabolism of the mind and develops a "funny mandala" called Brahm Mandala. This mudra is also good for outrageous behavior, deep depression and inconsistency in character. It creates happiness at the spot where there is unhappiness.

POSITION

1. Sit with your spine straight.

2. Your hands face each other at the level of your head and are held about 12 inches away from your face.

3. Make fists with both hands. Your thumbs are on the outside of your fists, with your index fingers pointing up.

4. Your left hand is lower, so that your left fingertip is exactly even with the lowest knuckle of your right thumb.

5. Your eyes are open, looking directly at and through the space between your hands.

This mudra symbolizes yin and yang pointing towards God. It is a mudra of immediate spirit and protection. All previous incarnations, the present and the future shall be directed towards righteousness.

MANTRA

Ad Guray Nameh
Jugad Guray Nameh
Sat Guray Nameh
Siri Guru Devay Nameh

Mentally meditate on this mantra for 11 minutes. Then close your eyes and chant aloud in a monotone. (Time unspecified)

COMMENTS

This mantra creates a sphere of protection from accidents and adversity. It translates as:

I bow to the primal Guru
I bow to the Wisdom through the Ages
I bow to the True Wisdom
I Bow to the Great Unseen Wisdom."

MEDITATION TO MELT NEGATIVITY

MUDRA

Sit in Easy Pose, with a straight spine. Bend the ring and pinkie fingers into the palm, and hold them down with the thumb. Extend the index and middle fingers straight up, and hold them side by side. Place this mudra about 2 feet to either side of the face, palms facing forward, fingers pointing up. The forearms and fingers will not be straight up towards the ceiling, but tilted out to the sides, at about a 30° angle. Keep the hands up at the level of the face. The elbows are bent, but not pressed into the sides of the body. They should be stretched out about 12 inches, away from the sides. The weight of the hands will be on the armpits. This allows the armpits to be open so they can breathe and be stimulated.

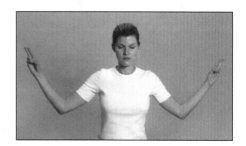

EYES

Either focus at the tip of your nose, or close the eyes—either way will work. However, if you look at the tip of the nose, then the third eye point will become heavy as lead, and if you can stand the pain, the third eye will open.

MANTRA

Aap Sahaa-ee Hoaa, Sachay Daa, Sachaa Dhoaa
Har(a), Har(a), Har(a)

Optional: tape by Singh Kaur is played. Chant along with the tape, from the navel. If not available, chant rhythmically.

CONDITIONS

To get the proper effect, as you chant the words **Har, Har, Har,** strike the tongue against the upper palate, and firmly pull in on the navel point on each repetition. This will pressurize the Kundalini, and shake it from the base.

TIME

27 minutes

END

Inhale deeply. Hold 23 seconds, and concentrate on the area from your navel to the crown chakra at the top of the head, or *shashaaraa*. This distance is only 27 inches. Exhale forcefully, like cannon fire. Repeat two more times, holding the breath only 5 seconds. Relax.

COMMENTS/EFFECTS

"This meditation melts negativity, enemies, and negative vibrations. It is such a powerful meditation that you can even go after a demon and make him a student.

"The armpits are the exhaust pipe of the brain. That's why the sweat in the armpits is very different than the sweat of the rest of the body. If the armpits do not sweat, you will have headaches. If you do not like the smell, put some sandalwood oil in your armpits. You will smell good, and in turn it will keep your brain fresh. If you become physically impotent, you can get an injection to correct it, but when you get mentally impotent, you are useless. Then you can't take care of yourself, your future, your environment, and your sensitivity."

This mantra takes your energy to the *shashaaraa*, the thousand-petal lotus, the crown chakra. It means, *The True God has come down as the True Helper, to uplift your Truth.* The 3 strokes of *Har* represent the *"Father, Son, and Holy Ghost"* or the three aspects of God, *"Brahma, Vishnu, and Mahesh."* This mantra opens you up so the Universe will open to you. It's a simple bargain.

MEDITATION FOR WHEN YOU DON'T KNOW WHAT TO DO

When you do not know what to do, try this meditation. It is very simple, but very powerful if done correctly. It coordinates both areas of the brain, gives you powerful insight and coordinates the mystery of the spiritual phenomena into the mastery of the three bodies (physical, mental, and spiritual). Though it looks simple, it solves many complications. It is sometimes called Gyan Mudra Kriya.

POSITION

Sit straight, either cross-legged or in a chair.

FOCUS

Look at the third eye point, then bring the eyes to the tip of the nose.

MUDRA

Relax the arms down by the side of the body. Bend the elbows and raise the hands up and in until they meet at the level of the chest. The fingers of each hand are extended and joined in a relaxed way. Cross the hands with both palms facing toward the chest. One palm rests in the other and the thumbs are crossed. The fingers point up at a comfortable angle. (The position of the left and right hands is interchangeable for this exercise.)

BREATH

Inhale through the nose, then exhale through the nose. Now, inhale through the mouth and exhale through the mouth. Next, inhale through the nose and exhale through the mouth. Finally, inhale through the mouth and exhale through the nose.

Continue this sequence. All breaths should be deep, complete and powerful. When breathing through the mouth, purse the lips almost as if to whistle.

TIME

Start practicing this kriya for 11 minutes and gradually increase the time to 31 minutes.

MEDITATION TO DO WHEN NOTHING ELSE WORKS

When you are at your wits end, when you do not know what to do, when nothing else works, this meditation does. This is one of the five meditations given specifically "to prepare for the gray period of the planet and to bring mental balance."

MUDRA

Make an inverted Venus lock—fingers are interlaced backwards. Hold at the solar plexus, palms facing up, fingers pointing up, thumbs straight. Eyes are ¹/₁₀th open.

MANTRA

Chant the *Guru Gaitri Mantra*:

> **Gobinday, Mukanday, Udaaray, Apaaray,
> Haring, Karing, Nirnamay, Akaamay**

It should totally turn into a sound current: Chant as fast as possible so that the words are indistinguishable.

TIME: Start with 11 minutes and build up 31 minutes.

MERCURY PERIOD

Meditations to bring out the beneficial aspects of Mercury

❋

Kabadshe Mantra

❋

Meditation For Stress

❋

Meditation For Stress or Sudden Shock

❋

Meditation For Strong Nerves

KABADSHE MANTRA

This is the base mantra of all mantras. SA is God. HAR is the Earth. You must perfect it before all others. Adversity can not stand before this mantra. If you focus on the mantra and tune, it will happen on the spot. As humans are the by-product of geography, God is the by-product of human will. We talk to each other through language, just as the Gods talk through their mantras.

This mantra combines Ether and Earth. It gives you the power of communication; therefore, your words shall have mastery and impact and shall be vital.

This mantra is used to conquer the wisdom of the past, present and future. Knowledge of the three worlds and all totality will come to the person who recites this mantra.

It will bring peace to those on whose forehead it is not written. It will bring prosperity to those who do not know how to spell it. It will bring you good luck when you have done nothing good, even in your dreams. It will bring peace, prosperity and luck, because this is the opening of the lotus and turning the Mother Divine power back to the navel point.

"I gave you this gift so that you can give it to your children, grandchildren, great-grandchildren, and specially to your old relatives who are on the way out but they do not know where to exit." —Yogi Bhajan

POSITION

Touch the thumb tip to the pinkie fingertip (Mercury). Rest hands on the knees with palms facing up.

MANTRA

Sa Re Sa Sa
Sa Re Sa Sa
Sa Re Sa Sa
Sarung

Har-re Har Har
Har-re Har Har
Har-re Har Har
Harung

TIME

Start with 11 minutes, build up to 31, then 62.

MEDITATION FOR STRESS

This meditation balances the western hemisphere of the brain with the base of the eastern hemisphere. This enables the brain to maintain its equilibrium under stress or weight of a sudden shock. It also keeps the nerves from being shattered under these circumstances.

POSITION
Sit with the legs crossed or in a chair with the weight of both feet equally distributed on the ground. The spine is straight. Focus at the tip of the nose.

ARMS AND HANDS
Right arm: Extend the right arm straight to the right, parallel to the ground with the elbow bent. Draw the forearm in toward the body until the hand is in front of the chest near the level of the throat. Extend and join the fingers. Face the palm toward the ground with the fingers pointing to the left.

Left arm: Draw the thumb back and down with the elbow bent. Draw the forearm straight up until it is directly in front of the upper arm with the left hand at the same height as the right hand. Extend and join the fingers. Bend the hand back to a 90° angle and face the palm up with the fingers also pointing to the left. Pull the thumb to the rear and point it back in the direction of the body. Do not move an inch once you are in the position.

BREATH

Deeply inhale and completely exhale as the mantra is chanted.

MANTRA

Chant the following mantra in a monotone voice as the breath is completely exhaled:

Sat Nam, Sat Nam, Sat Nam, Sat Nam
Sat Nam, Sat Nam, Wahe Guru

Sat Nam, Sat Nam, Sat Nam, Sat Nam
Sat Nam, Sat Nam, Wahe Guru

Sat Nam, Sat Nam, Sat Nam, Sat Nam
Sat Nam, Sat Nam, Wahe Guru

Sat Nam, Sat Nam, Sat Nam, Sat Nam
Sat Nam, Sat Nam, Wahe Guru

The entire mantra must be chanted on only **one** breath. The rhythm must be exact. Use the tip of the tongue to pronounce each word exactly.

END

Upon completion of the meditation deeply inhale and completely exhale 5 times. Then deeply inhale and hold the breath while the arms are stretched over the head as high as possible. Stretch with every ounce that can be mustered. Exhale and relax down. Repeat twice more with the stretch.

TIME

Begin with 11 minutes and slowly build up to 31 minutes.

MEDITATION FOR STRONG NERVES

Practice this meditation to gain a calm mind and strong nerves. It will help protect you from irrationality. This is one of five meditations given specifically "to prepare for the gray period of the planet and to bring mental balance."

POSITION

Sit with a straight spine. Eyes are $1/10$th open.

MUDRA

Hold the right hand at ear level with the thumb tip and ring finger tip touching (fingernails do not touch). Place the left hand in the lap with the thumb tip and tip of the pinkie fingers touching. Women should reverse the position so that the left hand has thumb and ring finger touching with hand at ear level, and the right hand is in the lap with the thumb and little finger touching.

BREATH

Make the breath long and deep but not powerful.

TIME

You can practice this meditation anywhere, starting with 11 minutes and working up to 31 minutes. To end the meditation inhale deeply, open the fingers, raise the hands and shake them rapidly for several minutes. Take some time to relax.

JUPITER PERIOD

Meditations to bring out the beneficial aspects of Jupiter

❀

Prosperity, Goodwill & Projection

❀

Subagh Kriya: For Prosperity

❀

Meditation for Mental Purity

❀

Meditation for Brosa

PROSPERITY, GOODWILL AND PROJECTION

POSITION

Sit with legs crossed or in any meditative pose. *Your spine must be kept absolutely straight.* The eyes are $1/10$th open.

MUDRA

1. Your hands meet at the level of the mouth. Your elbows are relaxed down. Your left palm faces your body and your right palm faces away. Extend your index fingers. The other fingers are folded into your palms.

2. Press your index fingertips together with 10–15 pounds of pressure per square inch. Be sure that your index fingers are slanted toward each other at such an angle that they create an equilateral triangle.

MANTRA

Chant rhythmically in a monotone.

Har Haray Haree
Wha-Hey Guru

TO END

Inhale deeply and shake your hands above your head. Relax.

TIME

Build up to 31 minutes.

SUBAGH KRIYA: MEDITATION FOR PROSPERITY

POSITION

Sit in Easy Pose with a straight spine. Eyes are focused at the tip of your nose. Relax your upper arms, bend the elbows and bring the palms facing up to the front of the chest.

1. Strike the outer sides of the hands together, forcefully hitting the area from the base of the little finger (Mercury finger) to the base of the palm. This area is called the Moon area. Palms face up.

2. Next, strike the sides of the index fingers (Jupiter fingers) together. Hit hard! Palms face down.

MANTRA

Alternately strike the Moon area and the Jupiter area as you chant **HAR** with the tip of the tongue. Chant powerfully from the navel, pulling the navel in with each HAR.

MUSIC

Optional: chant to Rootlight's *Soul Trance (Har)* or Simran Kaur Khalsa's *Tantric Har* tape.

MEDITATION FOR MENTAL PURITY

This meditation has the capacity to make your mind clear as a crystal. It can totally eliminate mental impurity, but it must be done correctly!

POSITION

Sit in a comfortable cross-legged sitting position, or sit in a chair with the weight of both feet equally distributed on the ground. Rest the right hand in the left with both palms facing up. The position is reversed if you are a woman. Point thumbs straight away from the body. Hold this position at the center of the chest at the bottom of the rib cage. The arms rest against the sides of the body with the elbows bent. The eyes are 1/10th open.

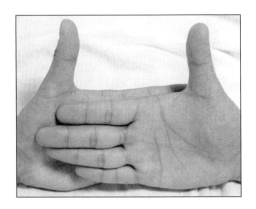

MANTRA

Begin chanting the following mantra:

Gobinde Gobinde Haree Haree
Gobinde Gobinde Haree Haree
Gobinde Gobinde Haree Haree
Gobinde Gobinde Haree Haree
Gobinde Gobinde Haree Haree

Continue the chant without any break, allowing the breath to regulate itself.

Go is pronounced like "go." *Bind* rhymes with "grinned." *Haree* is pronounced like "hurry," except that the "r" is a soft "r" as in the Spanish language, and the *ee* is held a bit longer than in the English language. This mantra is chanted in a monotone in a four-beat rhythm. As you say the syllable *Go*, pucker the lips, as if to kiss someone, *bind*, the tongue is pressed against the front teeth. As you say the word *Haree*, the lips will smile somewhat.

TIME
There is no restriction on the length of time for which this meditation can be practiced.

COMMENTS
In the coming times, many Americans will become nervous wrecks. They will not even be in a position to receive instruction in meditation. All you will be able to do for them is to put your hands over their heads and start chanting. This meditation will help to develop that healing power within you, provided you also perfect the mantra:

Sa-Ta-Na-Ma-Ra-Ma-Da-Sa-Sa-Say-So-Hung

MEDITATION FOR BROSA

This kriya is very potent and must be respected. The effects are extensive. The meditation affects the element of trust in the human personality. Trust is the basis of faith and commitment and the sense of reality. It will give you the elevation of spirit so you can stand up to any challenge. It builds and balances the aura from the fourth chakra up.

POSITION

Sit in lotus or Easy Pose. Arch the arms up over the head with the palms down. Men, put the right palm on top of the left. Women, put the left palm on top of the right. Put the thumb tips together with thumbs pointing back. The arms are bent at the elbows slightly. Keep the eyelids open slightly and look down toward the upper lip.

MANTRA

Chant the mantra **Wahe Guru**. Form the sounds with the lips and tongue very precisely. Whisper it so that the *Guru* is almost inaudible. It takes about 2 1/2 seconds per repetition.

TIME

Continue for 11 minutes. When beginning to experience this meditation, it should be done for a maximum of 11 minutes. Then increase the time by 1 minute after every 15 days of practice until you reach a total of 31 minutes.

VENUS PERIOD

Meditations to bring out the beneficial aspects of Venus

❋

Green Energy, Prosperity and
Stability in Relationships

❋

Relax and Rejoice

❋

Tranquilize the Mind

❋

Completely Neutralize Tension

❋

Kirtan Sohila: For the Breath of Life

MEDITATION FOR GREEN ENERGY, PROSPERITY, AND STABILITY IN RELATIONSHIPS

POSITION

Sit in a meditative pose with your spine straight. The hands are gently cupped with palms facing up. Place the right hand over the left with the thumbs touching and pointing away from the body.

MANTRA

Inhale and chant on the exhale, one cycle per breath.

Haree Haree Haree Haree
Haree Haree Harrr

The mantra is chanted in a monotone powerfully from the navel, with the stress placed on the last syllable.

TIME

Continue for 11–31 minutes.

MEDITATION TO RELAX AND REJOICE

This meditation will help you relax and rejoice. It enables you to understand the contrast between working from your ego and working from your inner self, the will of God, the soul.

POSITION

Sit in Easy Pose with a straight spine. Be relaxed.

MUDRA

Relax the arms down by the sides of the body with the elbows bent. Draw the forearms in toward each other until the hands meet in front of the body. Make a fist of the left hand and stick the thumb down into the middle of the fist. Wrap the right hand around the left fist and place the right thumb over the left fist on top of the base of the left thumb.

EYES

Focus on the tip of the nose.

MANTRA

Deeply inhale, then completely exhale as you chant the following mantra in a monotone voice:

Haree Har, Haree Har, Haree Har, Haree Har
Haree Har, Haree Har, Haree Har, Haree Har

TIME

Begin by practicing the meditation for 10–15 minutes and slowly build to 1 or 2 hours. This is a very spacey meditation, so practice it when you have time to relax after.

MEDITATION TO TRANQUILIZE THE MIND

POSITION

Sit in Easy Pose with the spine straight.

MUDRA

With the elbows bent, bring the hands up and in until they meet in front of the body at the level of the heart. The elbows should be held up almost to the level of the hands. Bend the index fingers of each hand in toward the palm. Join them with each other so they press together along the second joint. The middle fingers are extended and meet at the fingertips. The other fingers are curled into the hand. The thumbs meet at the fingertips. Hold the mudra about 4 inches from the body with the extended fingers pointing away from the body.

EYES

Focus on the tip of the nose. Inhale completely and hold the breath while repeating the mantra of your choice 11–21 times. Exhale, hold the breath out, and repeat the mantra an equal number of times.

TIME

Practice for 3 minutes.

MEDITATION TO COMPLETELY NEUTRALIZE TENSION

This is an extremely relaxing meditation. It completely neutralizes tension, and puts you in the most relaxing situation you can possibly imagine. By doing this meditation for 40 days, you can revitalize your glandular system and reestablish glandular equilibrium.

POSITION
Sit in Easy Pose with the spine straight.

MUDRA

1. From a relaxed position at the sides of the body, bend at the elbows and bring the forearms up and in toward each other until the hands meet at the heart level.

2. Face both palms up and cross the right palm over the left palm with the fingers extended and joined. Place the left thumb in the center of the right palm and cross the right thumb over the left thumb.

MANTRA
Deeply inhale and completely exhale as you chant.

Sa-a-a-a-a-a-at Naam

EYES
The eyes are $1/10$th open. As the meditation progresses, they may close all the way.

TIME
Begin with 11 minutes and build up to 31 minutes.

KIRTAN SOHILA: FOR THE BREATH OF LIFE AND TO MAKE LIFE HEALTHY AND PURE

By doing this before you go to sleep at night, it will bring about a beneficial change in your destiny. It brings the neutrality of the tattwas (five elements). Each dawn will bring a message of freshness and new opportunities.

POSITION

Sit in Easy Pose with the spine straight. Hands are in prayer pose at the heart. Make sure the palms stay pressed together. Eyes are 1/10th open gently focused at the tip of the nose.

BREATH

Inhale deeply and hold the breath. Mentally repeat **Wahe Guru** rhythmically 8 times. *Exhale* completely and hold the breath. Mentally repeat **Wahe Guru** 8 times.

TIME

11–31 minutes at night before bed.

SATURN PERIOD

Meditations to bring out the beneficial aspects of Saturn

❋

Modify the Negative Influences of Saturn

❋

Maturity and Wisdom

❋

For the Arcline and to Clear the Karmas

❋

To Develop Will Power and Self-understanding

MODIFY THE NEGATIVE INFLUENCES OF SATURN

POSITION

Sit with legs crossed, spine straight. The eyes are focused at the tip of the nose. The arms are bent at the elbows and raised parallel to the floor almost at the level of the chin. Keep shoulders relaxed.

MUDRA

The palms face down, the left hand on top of the right. The fingers are inter-laced, except for the Saturn (middle) fingers, which point down, with pads touching so that a lock is created. The thumbs touch tip to tip.

MANTRA

The mantra is chanted in a monotone powerfully from the navel, with the stress placed on the last syllable. Two cycles are chanted on each breath, 12 seconds per repetition (including the inhale).

Haree Haree Haree Haree
Haree Haree Haree Harrr

TIME

The recommended time is 31 minutes.

MEDITATION FOR MATURITY AND WISDOM

POSITION

Bend your elbows to your waist and
extend the forearms up so the palms are
a few inches in front of each shoulder,
palms flat and facing the body. Then
bend the palms back slightly at the
wrist, until the palms are facing up, and
are somewhat relaxed and somewhat
cupped. Hold this position.

EYES: Stare at the tip of the nose.

MOVEMENT

Without using the breath in any specific way, begin to pump the
navel point powerfully. Pump very hard and very fast, but it is not
Breath of Fire.

TIME: 31 minutes

END

Inhale, and pump the navel vigorously. Hold 10 seconds. Exhale.
Repeat 3 times total. Relax.

COMMENTS/EFFECTS

Your handicaps travel ahead of you, and your reputation is known
before you even reach a place. So it is very beautiful for people to
drop their past, change their attitude, have the altitude, and make
sense to themselves. Then everybody can be sensibly made to understand that you are beautiful, bountiful and blissful, trustworthy,
gracious, with divinity and dignity, and you can be a friend unto
infinity. You must understand: there is no prize which can give you
back your honor.

MEDITATION FOR THE ARCLINE AND TO CLEAR THE KARMAS

POSITION

Sit in Easy Pose with a straight spine. Eyes are closed.

1. Touch the elbows to the waist while stretching the forearms out in front of the body, palms slightly cupped and facing up. Place them a few inches above the knees.

2. Bring arms up, back behind head, stretching hands and arms as far back over shoulders as you can. Imagine you are scooping water, and throwing it through your arcline, over your shoulders, with a flick of the wrists. The movement is smooth and gracefully flows along with the lyrics and rhythm of the music.

MANTRA

Wahe Guru
Wahe Guru
Wahe Guru
Wahe Jio

Either listen to *Wahe Guru, Wahe Guru, Wahe Guru, Wahe Jio* (*Soul Trance* CD is available from Rootlight) or chant in a rhythmic monotone. On each "Wa-hay Guroo," as well as on the "Wa-hay Jeeo," do one complete round-scooping up, throwing over your shoulders, and come back to the starting position.

TIME
31 minutes

END
Inhale, and stretch your hands back as far as possible, hands right behind your head, posture for the inhale must be correct. Hold 10–15 seconds. Exhale. Repeat 3 times total. Relax.

COMMENTS
This meditation is for the arcline and to clear the karma that has been stocked up in it. You'll experience what *Wahe Guru* actually means. Remember, the power of infinity is not outside of you—it is inside of you. When "I" and infinity create impact, you'll become totally divine. Otherwise there's a duality which keeps you away from reality, and the pain is tremendous.

TAPA YOG KARAM KRIYA:
TO DEVELOP WILL POWER AND SELF-UNDERSTANDING

POSITION

Sit in a meditative pose. Extend the arms straight forward, parallel to the ground. Palms face each other. Put the wrists together. Then spread the palms out as far as you can, as though pushing against a wall.

EYES

The eyes are slightly open looking down at the tip of the nose.

MANTRA: Begin rhythmically chanting

Sat Nam, Sat Nam, Sat Nam, Sat Nam,
Sat Nam, Sat Nam, Wa-hay Guru

TIME

11 minutes

COMMENTS

We cannot improve the caliber of the human being, but we can guide it. When we guide ourselves and are not at the mercy of subconscious habits, then we become master of the self. But overcoming old habits and starting new ones requires strong nerves and will power. This kriya develops will power and gives the capacity to understand the elements of your personality. You can know what you are thinking and regulate the flow of these thoughts. This kriya is a perfect sadhana for difficulty in completing projects and doing what you intend.

Saturn, Mars and Your Health

It is vital to be more health-conscious than usual in the Saturn and Mars periods. During these times, you are more susceptible to infectious diseases than in others. Therefore, not only should you pay attention to rebuilding and improving your health, but you should also stay away from any situation or person that may cause you to be sick.

Since these periods are very challenging, it is easier to experience chronic stress. Needless to say, stress is very unhealthy. Anxiety, stress and fear squeeze the nerves, which then prevent the free transport of prana. Consequently, energy is blocked and particular organs are weakened. Since the nerves receive energy from the cosmos, which in turn feeds the muscles and organs, they are extremely important in distributing prana throughout the body.

One of the first common signs of stress is skin disorders, such as rashes, eczema and so forth. If this condition persists, one or more of the organs may not be receiving an ample amount of prana. The body is then weakened and serious health problems, such as cancer, can ensue.

Skin disorders can be prevented or improved by altering your lifestyle, and importantly, by understanding the following: The spleen and liver are extremely important. Above all, the etheric spleen (the energy counterpart of the physical spleen) is responsible for the absorption and transmutation of prana from the Sun, so that it may be distributed throughout the body. If the etheric spleen is weak, prana cannot be distributed properly, and the health of the body suffers.

Throughout centuries of research, yogis have discovered particular meditations to keep the spleen, as well as the liver, functioning properly. One such meditation uses the science of breath. It is called *Sitali Pranayam*. This particular breath is known to lengthen one's life span, because it increases the amount of life force in the body. This cooling breath helps the spleen, liver and digestive system. It is very beneficial in lowering fevers and overall body temperature. It regulates the sexual energy, helps digestion, and is good for detoxification of the body. Heaven serves those who practice this breath, for the things they need come to them. You can enhance the benefits of this breath by filling the lower part of the lungs when inhaling through your rolled tongue and exhaling through the nose. It will re-energize the natural path linking the nervous connections and muscles. Breathing very long and deep will not only give great benefit, but it also can eliminate neck pain and adjust the jaw. It also works on the throat chakra, which is the center of communication and projection. The following meditation and foot bath are recommended for the Mars and Saturn periods, because they will cool the fire of Mars and keep the earthly body balanced. They can be used at any other time to maintain vibrant health.

 ## MEDITATION TO IMPROVE THE FUNCTION OF THE SPLEEN AND LIVER: SITALI PRANAYAM

POSITION

Sit in a comfortable position with the spine straight. Hands are either relaxed on lap, or you can spread the fingers and touch the fingertips of both hands together at the level of the solar plexus (between heart and navel). This hand position seals in the energy, so it can be contained and used for healing. Close the eyes and focus at the brow point.

BREATH

Inhale through a curled tongue, as if you are sipping through a straw. Hold the breath for as long as possible. Exhale slowly through the nose. Continue the breath cycle.

TIME: Start with at least 11 minutes. There is no time limit.

Footbath for Relaxation and Renewal

Here is another simple and powerful method to calm and revitalize the nerves, open blocked channels, and strengthen the spleen, liver and glands. We have 72,000 nerves, which are the transporters of prana. These nerves end in our feet and hands. Every organ has a corresponding spot on the soles of the feet. Therefore, massaging the feet relaxes the nerves and creates a healing effect on the body. You can prevent many health disorders, heal vital organs, and strengthen the immune system by doing the following:

The items you will need are
• **sea salt**
• **eucalyptus oil**
• **hot water**

1. Fill the bathtub or a bucket with enough hot water (not scalding) to at least cover your ankles.

2. Add sea salt (to draw out impurities) and eucalyptus oil (to calm and soothe the nerves).

3. Sit down on a chair and place feet into the water. For the first 3 minutes, massage your feet with your hands. Then sit back and relax for an additional 8 minutes.

4. Remove feet and dry them. Optional: Massage feet with oil or lotion.

5. If you so desire, this is a good time to go to your meditation place and do Sitali Pranayam for a minimum of 11 minutes.

This healing footbath, followed by Sitali Pranayam is best done at the end of the day. However, you may do it anytime you choose.

✦ THE ART OF ABSENT HEALING

The purpose of this technique is to render spiritual healing to a person you know who is in distress—a member of your family, a friend, a neighbor, or anyone who is afflicted by a physical, mental or material problem.

PREPARATION

When you have selected the person in need of healing, close your eyes and take a few deep breaths to quiet your mind and go within. Now say the following prayer:

"Divine Intelligence, purify my whole being so I may be a perfect channel for healing energy. So be it."

STEP ONE

Start with the 3-point breath (inhale for count of 20, hold for 20, exhale for 20). Sit in a meditative position with the spine straight. Hands are in prayer pose, palms pressed together at the level of the chest and thumbs against the sternum. *(3–11 minutes)*

STEP TWO: MEDITATION FOR SELF-HEALING

This mantra heals all imbalances and sickness. Place palms facing each other 6 inches apart at the level of the heart. Eyes are closed. Inhale, hold the breath for a few seconds, and as you exhale, chant the mantra up the major scale (as in Do, Re, Mi, Fa, So, La, Ti, Do) or you can order the RaMaDaSa healing CD from the back of this book and work with it. The mantra is: *Ra—Ma—Da—Sa—Sa—Say—So—Hung*

1. Sing the mantra aloud for 11 minutes.

2. Whisper the mantra for 5 minutes.

3. Listen to the vibration of the mantra inside you, silently for one minute. To end, inhale, hold the breath, and surround yourself with the healing light of the Sun. Then exhale. Do this three times. *(Pause for approximately one minute before continuing to the next step.)*

STEP THREE: SEND HEALING

1. Visualize as vividly as possible the person who needs your help. Then imagine the person sitting completely receptive. *(Pause)*

2. While in this receptive state, picture a light that slowly beams down from the sun and surrounds the person. *(Pause)*

3. As the light intensifies around the person, feel their entire being gradually becoming charged and vibrating with strength, health and harmony. *(Pause)*

4. Visualize the person happy, smiling, laughing, joking, being their best, and vibrating with health. *(Pause)*

5. While maintaining this visualization, inhale, hold the breath and mentally say, *"It is done."* Exhale.

6. Now forget the face of the person and say, *"Divine Intelligence, bless my work. So be it."* *(Pause)*

Go back to your daily activities. Your may draw your inspiration from this simple ritual, performing it anytime of the day, shaping it to your liking, and adding any other elements you may deem necessary.

The process of self-healing is the privilege of every human being.

Self-healing is not a miracle, nor is it a question of being able to do something that most people can't.

Self-healing is a process that occurs through the relationship between the physical and the infinite power of the soul.

*It is a contract, a union
—that is the science of Kundalini yoga.*

—Yogi Bhajan

Chapter Ten

The Seven Creative Planets
and the Days of the Week

To recapitulate, each of the seven periods are governed by the seven planets: Sun, Moon, Mars, Mercury, Jupiter, Venus and Saturn. The days of the week have been named after the seven creative planets. Sunday, Monday, Tuesday, Wednesday, Thursday, Friday and Saturday are ruled, respectively, by the Sun, Moon, Mars, Mercury, Jupiter, Venus and Saturn. In other words, the same planetary order used in the seven periods is also used for the seven days of the week. Both start with the Sun.

The Daily Ruling Planets

SUNDAY is ruled by the Sun.

The Sun stands for royalty, expansion, travel, growth, health, vitality, feasts, the heart and spirituality. This is a day for regeneration and to express the divine self. It is easy to reach illumination on this day. Your Sunday is a good day to ask for a raise at work, improve your mind, and deal with money matters.

MONDAY is ruled by the Moon.

The Moon stands for imagination, dreams, intuition, women, relationships, change, public life and digestion. This is the best time to improve your feelings and behavior. One can use Monday to mend a broken love relationship or to deal with public life. It is, above all, an emotional day. What you do on Monday can determine your future, either positively or negatively. The electromagnetic field in the brain works best on Monday. Therefore, it is the best time for doing visualization to uplift the circumstances in your life.

TUESDAY is ruled by Mars.

Mars stands for war, violence, conflict, accidents, fire, action, will power and physical strength. Any time that you need additional strength and energy to accomplish a task, do it on Tuesday. Mars is the planet that governs policemen, surgeons and athletes. It is the best day to exercise and work out. Also, it is the best day to meet your adversaries and face obstacles. You can chose your own terms on this day.

WEDNESDAY is ruled by Mercury.

Mercury stands for travel, communication, writing, commerce, journalism, healers and jewelers. It is the best time to write letters and communicate with whomever. The best time to study is on Wednesday, because the mind is more receptive to assimilation on this day.

THURSDAY is ruled by Jupiter.

Jupiter stands for prosperity, banking, politics, law, values, hotels, restaurants/food, glory and honor. This is the best time to crystallize your wishes. You can get in touch with higher authorities for help on this day. It is also a good time to borrow money. Thursday is a day for expansion, deep thought and absolute wisdom. It is a lucky day; therefore it is difficult to make a mistake on Thursdays.

FRIDAY is ruled by Venus.

Venus stands for love, beauty, arts, fashion and perfume. Most people are open to love on this day, so it is the best time for romance. If you purchase your clothes and beauty products on Friday, many people will like your choices.

SATURDAY is ruled by Saturn.

Saturn stands for law, justice, institutions, savings, mines, discipline and restriction. It is the best time to write to law authorities. It is difficult to accomplish things on this day. You can resolve a problem with a violent person on Saturday. Be cool and lay low.

Regarding Your Personal Week

There are tides in human affairs. When those tides are taken into consideration during any transactions, you can become extremely fortunate. <u>There are general and personal weeks</u>. The general one is what we all follow all over the world, and as you know, it starts on Sunday and ends on Saturday. In order to conduct your daily affairs effectively, just remember that the most fortunate days are Sunday, Thursday and Friday. This is a general rule, so it will not apply to everyone.

If you find that these days do not work for you, it is because we are all born on different days of the week. It is very important to know which day of the week you were born. If you were born on Sunday, you will be successful on the days mentioned above. If you were not, find your personal week, which actually begins on your day of birth. In other words, if Thursday is your day of birth in the *general* week, it becomes Sunday in your *personal* week. In your case, Thursday, Monday and Tuesday from the *general* week respectively become in your *personal* week Sunday, Thursday and Friday. On those days, the tides are in your favor.

Following is a chart which will help determine your day of birth to allow you to find your ruling planet. The original chart was given to me by the English genealogist Dorothea Dore. She acquired it during the course of her genealogical studies over a period of twenty years. She is a member of the Association of Professional Genealogists and Record Agents in England. I have made a few adjustments for the purpose of this book and other publications.

Guide to Determine Day of Birth

STEP 1: Select year desired, obtain letter as key.
STEP 2: With key and month desired, obtain number of true month.
STEP 3: With true month number and day desired, determine the
       day of the week.

Example: Date desired is July 20, 1903.
1) KEY is H.   2) TRUE MONTH is 15.   3) DAY is Monday.

STEP 1: Obtain key for selected year
Calendar from 1881 to 2008

1881 J	1900 N	1919 L	1938 J	1957 K	1976 F	1995 M
1882 M	1901 K	1920 F	1939 M	1958 L	1977 J	1996 D
1883 N	1902 L	1921 J	1940 D	1959 H	1978 M	1997 L
1884 G	1903 H	1922 M	1941 L	1960 B	1979 N	1998 H
1885 H	1904 B	1923 N	1942 H	1961 M	1980 G	1999 I
1886 I	1905 M	1924 G	1943 I	1962 N	1981 H	2000 E
1887 J	1906 N	1925 H	1944 E	1963 K	1982 I	2001 N
1888 A	1907 K	1926 I	1945 N	1964 C	1983 J	2002 K
1889 K	1908 C	1927 J	1946 K	1965 I	1984 A	2003 L
1890 L	1909 I	1928 A	1947 L	1966 J	1985 K	2004 F
1891 H	1910 J	1929 K	1948 F	1967 M	1986 L	2005 J
1892 B	1911 M	1930 L	1949 J	1968 D	1987 H	2006 M
1893 M	1912 D	1931 H	1950 M	1969 L	1988 B	2007 N
1894 N	1913 L	1932 B	1951 N	1970 H	1989 M	2008 G
1895 K	1914 H	1933 M	1952 G	1971 I	1990 N	
1896 C	1915 I	1934 N	1953 H	1972 E	1991 K	
1897 I	1916 E	1935 K	1954 I	1973 N	1992 C	
1898 J	1917 N	1936 C	1955 J	1974 K	1993 I	
1899 M	1918 K	1937 I	1956 A	1975 L	1994 J	

STEP 2: Use key to obtain True Month

	A	B	C	D	E	F	G
JAN	18	20	15	17	19	14	16
FEB	1	3	12	28	2	4	27
MAR	14	16	18	20	15	17	19
APRIL	25	13	22	24	26	21	23
MAY	16	18	20	15	17	19	14
JUNE	13	22	24	26	21	23	25
JULY	18	20	15	17	19	14	16
AUG	15	17	19	14	16	18	20
SEPT	26	21	23	25	13	22	24
OCT	17	19	14	16	18	20	15
NOV	21	23	25	13	22	24	26
DEC	19	14	16.	18	20	15	17
	A	B	C	D	E	F	G

Leap Years

	H	I	J	K	L	M	N
JAN	14	20	19	16	15	18	17
FEB	11	10	9	6	5	8	7
MAR	18	17	16	20	19	15	14
APRIL	22	21	13	24	23	26	25
MAY	20	19	18	15	14	17	16
JUNE	24	23	22	26	25	21	13
JULY	15	14	20	17	16	19	18
AUG	19	18	17	14	20	16	15
SEPT	23	22	21	25	24	13	26
OCT	14	20	19	16	15	18	17
NOV	25	24	23	13	26	22	21
DEC	16	15	14	18	17	20	19
	H	I	J	K	L	M	N

Common Years

STEP 3: Obtain day of the week

No. 1

Su	M	T	W	Th	F	Sa
			1	2	3	4
5	6	7	8	9	10	11
12	13	14	15	16	17	18
19	20	21	22	23	24	25
26	27	28	29			

No. 2

Su	M	T	W	Th	F	Sa
		1	2	3	4	5
6	7	8	9	10	11	12
13	14	15	16	17	18	19
20	21	22	23	24	25	26
27	28	29				

No. 3

Su	M	T	W	Th	F	Sa
	1	2	3	4	5	6
7	8	9	10	11	12	13
14	15	16	17	18	19	20
21	22	23	24	25	26	27
28	29					

No. 4

Su	M	T	W	Th	F	Sa
1	2	3	4	5	6	7
8	9	10	11	12	13	14
15	16	17	18	19	20	21
22	23	24	25	26	27	28
29						

No. 5

Su	M	T	W	Th	F	Sa
						1
2	3	4	5	6	7	8
9	10	11	12	13	14	15
16	17	18	19	20	21	22
23	24	25	26	27	28	

No. 6

Su	M	T	W	Th	F	Sa
					1	2
3	4	5	6	7	8	9
10	11	12	13	14	15	16
17	18	19	20	21	22	23
24	25	26	27	28		

No. 7

Su	M	T	W	Th	F	Sa
				1	2	3
4	5	6	7	8	9	10
11	12	13	14	15	16	17
18	19	20	21	22	23	24
25	26	27	28			

No. 8

Su	M	T	W	Th	F	Sa
			1	2	3	4
5	6	7	8	9	10	11
12	13	14	15	16	17	18
19	20	21	22	23	24	25
26	27	28				

No. 9

Su	M	T	W	Th	F	Sa
		1	2	3	4	5
6	7	8	9	10	11	12
13	14	15	16	17	18	19
20	21	22	23	24	25	26
27	28					

No. 10

Su	M	T	W	Th	F	Sa
	1	2	3	4	5	6
7	8	9	10	11	12	13
14	15	16	17	18	19	20
21	22	23	24	25	26	27
28						

No. 11

Su	M	T	W	Th	F	Sa
1	2	3	4	5	6	7
8	9	10	11	12	13	14
15	16	17	18	19	20	21
22	23	24	25	26	27	28

No. 12

Su	M	T	W	Th	F	Sa
						1
2	3	4	5	6	7	8
9	10	11	12	13	14	15
16	17	18	19	20	21	22
23	24	25	26	27	28	29

No. 13

Su	M	T	W	Th	F	Sa
					1	2
3	4	5	6	7	8	9
10	11	12	13	14	15	16
17	18	19	20	21	22	23
24	25	26	27	28	29	30

No. 14

Su	M	T	W	Th	F	Sa
				1	2	3
4	5	6	7	8	9	10
11	12	13	14	15	16	17
18	19	20	21	22	23	24
25	26	27	28	29	30	31

No. 15

Su	M	T	W	Th	F	Sa
			1	2	3	4
5	6	7	8	9	10	11
12	13	14	15	16	17	18
19	20	21	22	23	24	25
26	27	28	29	30	31	

No. 16

Su	M	T	W	Th	F	Sa
	1	2	3	4	5	
6	7	8	9	10	11	12
13	14	15	16	17	18	19
20	21	22	23	24	25	26
27	28	29	30	31		

No. 17

Su	M	T	W	Th	F	Sa
	1	2	3	4	5	6
7	8	9	10	11	12	13
14	15	16	17	18	19	20
21	22	23	24	25	26	27
28	29	30	31			

No. 18

Su	M	T	W	Th	F	Sa
1	2	3	4	5	6	7
8	9	10	11	12	13	14
15	16	17	18	19	20	21
22	23	24	25	26	27	28
29	30	31				

No. 19

Su	M	T	W	Th	F	Sa
						1
2	3	4	5	6	7	8
9	10	11	12	13	14	15
16	17	18	19	20	21	22
23	24	25	26	27	28	29
30	31					

No. 20

Su	M	T	W	Th	F	Sa
					1	2
3	4	5	6	7	8	9
10	11	12	13	14	15	16
17	18	19	20	21	22	23
24	25	26	27	28	29	30
31						

No. 21

Su	M	T	W	Th	F	Sa
				1	2	3
4	5	6	7	8	9	10
11	12	13	14	15	16	17
18	19	20	21	22	23	24
25	26	27	28	29	30	

No. 22

Su	M	T	W	Th	F	Sa
			1	2	3	4
5	6	7	8	9	10	11
12	13	14	15	16	17	18
19	20	21	22	23	24	25
26	27	28	29	30		

No. 23

Su	M	T	W	Th	F	Sa
	1	2	3	4	5	
6	7	8	9	10	11	12
13	14	15	16	17	18	19
20	21	22	23	24	25	26
27	28	29	30			

No. 24

Su	M	T	W	Th	F	Sa
	1	2	3	4	5	6
7	8	9	10	11	12	13
14	15	16	17	18	19	20
21	22	23	24	25	26	27
28	29	30				

No. 25

Su	M	T	W	Th	F	Sa
1	2	3	4	5	6	7
8	9	10	11	12	13	14
15	16	17	18	19	20	21
22	23	24	25	26	27	28
29	30					

No. 26

Su	M	T	W	Th	F	Sa
						1
2	3	4	5	6	7	8
9	10	11	12	13	14	15
16	17	18	19	20	21	22
23	24	25	26	27	28	29
30						

No. 27

Su	M	T	W	Th	F	Sa
					1	2
3	4	5	6	7	8	9
10	11	12	13	14	15	16
17	18	19	20	21	22	23
24	25	26	27	28	29	

No.28

Su	M	T	W	Th	F	Sa
				1	2	3
4	5	6	7	8	9	10
11	12	13	14	15	16	17
18	19	20	21	22	23	24
25	26	27	28	29		

Your Primary Ruling Planet

Your primary ruling planet is determined by the day of the week you were born. This is your master key. Although there are various ways of finding the day of the week you were born, I recommend that you consult the previous chart or an ephemeris. The seven creative planets rule every possible vibration. The Sun, Jupiter and Venus are very beneficent planets, whereas Mars and Saturn are very challenging. The Moon and Mercury are considered neutral.

SUN

All the planets travel around the Sun at different speeds and distances. They distribute abilities and intelligence to individuals, depending on their angles and positions toward the Sun at our time of birth and throughout our lives. The Sun is 864,000 miles in diameter, ten times the width of Jupiter. Everything in our horoscope revolves around the Sun, and our whole essence comes from the position of the Sun at our birth. It marks the basic character of our personal radiation and will. It is a symbol of wisdom, dignity, strength and vigor. It is consciousness of the gift of life.

The Sun gives you highly creative energy. This aspect will give you all the courage, confidence, will and self-love it takes to be successful in your endeavors. The Sun will make you ambitious, proud and generous. Sun people love to be the center of attention. You will be outgoing and warm. Avoid becoming too self-involved and domineering. Those born with the Sun often leave their mark behind in the world.

MOON

The Moon is the planet of imagination and the subconscious. It will make you very emotional. In other words, you feel your way through life. You often fluctuate, thus making decisions difficult. You are dreamy and benefit psychologically by being around water.

People born under the vibration of the Moon can amass great wealth, but they have a hard time holding on to it, because they like to spend and give. It is very important to develop a healthy sense of giving, and be aware of over-identification and over-attachments. Avoid inconsistency, indecision, moodiness and gullibility. Master the process of your mind and stay positive.

MARS

Mars is about half the size of the Earth and it takes two years to orbit the Sun. It symbolizes raw, crude energy and represents the way we go for new adventure and experiences. Mars gives us energy and courage; initiative and daring. It influences war and anger; impulses and destruction.

Mars represents initiative, ambition, energy, courage and transformation. Mars gives great strength of individuality and independence. This vibration produces a person who is action-oriented and has an abundance of energy. Mars people can be outspoken and dictative in their behavior, which can create distressing conditions in domestic life. The challenging aspect of Mars represents war, internal and external struggles, desire, impulse and aggression. It can make one abrupt and possibly reckless. A person with Mars can not get away with impulsive, irresponsible behavior, because Mars people learn the hard way. Therefore, it is best to think before acting, rather than acting or speaking on impulse. There is a tendency for quick emotional flare-ups, which usually dissipate as quickly as they arise. The greatest challenge is to relax.

MERCURY

All the planets revolve around the Sun in oval patterns, and Mercury is the most elliptical in orbit, which means its distance from the Sun varies from twenty-nine million miles at its closest point and forty-three million miles at its farthest point. It is a small planet of 3,100 miles wide and takes eighty-eight days to orbit the Sun. Mercury represents our capacity to understand the desires of our own will and translate them into action. Mercury is the planet of mind and communication. Through Mercury we develop the abilities of thinking, writing and speaking.

Mercury stands for communication, perception and intellect. It will give you an incredibly active, logical and analytical mind, and a canny ability to see the humor and absurd side of situations. Mercury will also give you a quick mind and a special way with words. You can excel in all forms of communication, and will do well dealing with information. It is very important to avoid worrying and learn to relax.

JUPITER

Jupiter takes about twelve years to orbit the Sun. It is the largest planet in our solar system—nearly 90,000 miles in diameter—and almost 500 million miles from the Sun. Jupiter rules luck, wealth, happiness, optimism, success and joy. It is the symbol of opportunity and it opens the way for new possibilities in our lives. It rules all forms of expansion and gives us a thirst for knowledge and spiritual learning.

Jupiter is in charge of health, fortune, success, prosperity, and happiness. It is known as The Lord of Lords—the greatest of all planets. It rules expansion, travel, justice, religion, higher values and morality. Your fair and diplomatic ways are attributed to Jupiter. Spirituality will stimulate your interest. You will benefit from anything that is expansive, especially travel. Your warmth and generosity will open doors for you. You need to maintain moderation when it comes to food.

VENUS

Venus is almost as large as Earth. It is the nearest planet to Earth in the solar system and at times is only twenty-four million miles away from Earth. It takes 255 days to orbit the Sun and its cloud laden atmosphere reflects the sunlight and makes it outshine all the other planets. It symbolizes harmony, beauty, grace and balance. Venus endows us with our sense of beauty and love, <u>its ideal is the flame of spiritual love.</u>

Venus is the planet of harmony, beauty and love. Venus rules art, music, dance, theater, beauty, luxury and fashion. Although you may not be an artist yourself, Venus will give you love and appreciation for art and aesthetics. You will be concerned with luxury, sensuality, and social affairs. Venus can make you very romantic and often a bit indulgent. You may like to decorate, design, and beautify yourself and your surroundings. Venus will give you refinement and a sense of style. It can make you graceful and sociable. (You should avoid being vain, promiscuous, unfaithful, inconstant or overly materialistic. Many of your challenges in life will come through relationships with the opposite sex.)

true dat.

SATURN

Saturn is 800 million miles from the Earth and is the most beautiful from the solar system's planets with a set of magnificent rings made up of rock, ice crystals, and dust which reflect the light from the Sun. The rings are about 41,000 miles and ten miles thick. Saturn represents challenges, responsibilities and problems to be solved, and it causes delays and obstacles. It brings order and imposes reason. It shows us the consequences of being human and makes us accept the change and inevitable things that happen in human life. It also rules time and old age.

Saturn is the planet of karma, order, discipline, reason, rules, laws, limitation and obstacles. Saturn's energy is contractive. It is related to organization, structure, responsibility, ambition and perseverance. It will give you an organizing mind and make you a master of structure and form. It requires caution, restraint, focus and concentration. You will be strengthened by challenge and persistence. Avoid being melancholic or overly authoritative; learn to laugh and lighten up. You may experience delays, restriction, struggle, anxiety and fears that are unnecessary. Most great teachers are born under Saturn. A person with Saturn can not get away with frivolous, irresponsible behavior, because Saturn people pay for their actions and learn the hard way. Therefore, it is important to lead a clean life.

THE OUTER PLANETARY BODIES
The three outer planets must also be briefly acknowledged here for your information and reference.

Uranus was discovered in 1791. It is about sixty times the size of the Earth and takes eighty-four years to orbit the Sun. It rules unexpected change, revolution. It indicates latent originality and genius. It governs great leaps forward and always turns things around at the last minute and causes things to arrive out of nowhere.

Neptune was discovered in 1846 and takes 165 years to orbit the Sun. It is a very cold planet with a surface temperature of about -110° centigrade. Its effects on us are subtle, and it suggests a higher reality that we cannot describe, only feel, and it often makes feelings of guilt and worry apparent. Neptune is associated with all forms of escapism. As it is a planet of illusion, it governs the invisible realms which are beyond our ordinary day-to-day existence. Deceit, disappointment and disillusionment are all linked to Neptune.

Pluto was discovered in 1930 and takes 248 years to orbit the Sun. It appears to have no atmosphere, and frozen methane covers its surface. It rules in our horoscopes the passing of major milestones, and because of its distance, its effect are subtle and powerful. It creates and destroys, then creates again and slowly but surely changes things around so as to bring about a total transformation. Pluto rules the head and the powerful forces of creation and destruction that go on around us. It can change things totally and forever.

The Hourly Ruling Planets

It is important for you to know that the seven planets not only rule the yearly periods and the weekly days, but also the daily hours. *It must be emphasized that the order of the planets changes when applied to the hours.*

You must first have a clear understanding of the planetary order. The order of the planets ruling the hours comes from the Tree of Life, with the Earth as the center of the Universe.

1. Saturn   2. Jupiter   3. Mars   4. Sun   5. Venus   6. Mercury   7. Moon

There are 24 hours in a day, with the first hour being from 12:00 a.m. to 1:00 a.m., and seven days in a week. Each weekly day is ruled by a planet. The first hour of each day is governed by the ruling planet of that day. Therefore, the first hour of Sunday is ruled by the Sun, the first hour of Monday is ruled by the Moon, the first hour of Tuesday is ruled by Mars, and so on.

On Sunday, for instance, the first seven hours are ruled, respectively, by the **Sun**, *Venus, Mercury, Moon, Saturn, Jupiter, Mars*, and back to the *Sun*, keeping this descending order until the 24th hour. Similarly, the first seven hours of Saturday are ruled by **Saturn**, *Jupiter, Mars, Sun, Venus, Mercury, Moon*, and back to *Saturn*.

You may find it helpful to build a table of the week with the planetary hours. By doing so, you will easily understand how the planetary hours fluctuate from day to day, and you will be able to use it as a quick reference guide. There are four hours in a day that are all governed by the ruling planet of the day. They are the 1st, 8th, 15th, and 22nd hours. Here are the most auspicious hours:

SUNDAY ++ (+)	MONDAY + (0)	TUESDAY 0 (−)	WED. + (0)	THURS. ++ (+)	FRIDAY ++ (+)
12:00–2:00 AM	2:00–3:00 AM	1:00–3:00 AM	1:00–2:00 AM	12:00–1:00 AM	12:00–1:00 AM
5:00–6:00	6:00–7:00	6:00–7:00	3:00–4:00	2:00–4:00	4:00–5:00
7:00–9:00	9:00–10:00	8:00–10:00	8:00–9:00	5:00–6:00	6:00–8:00
12:00–1:00 PM	1:00–2:00 PM	1:00–2:00 PM	10:00–11:00	7:00–8:00	11:00–12:00
2:00–4:00	4:00–5:00	3:00–5:00	3:00–4:00 PM	9:00–11:00	1:00–3:00 PM
7:00–8:00	8:00–9:00	8:00–9:00	5:00–6:00	12:00–1:00 PM	6:00–7:00
9:00–11:00	11:00–12:00	10:00–12:00	10:00–11:00	2:00–3:00	8:00–10:00
				4:00–6:00	
				7:00–8:00	SAT. **0 (−)**
				9:00–10:00	none
				11:00–12:00	

KEY FOR DAYS: ++ very positive   + positive   0 neutral   − negative   ( ) waning moon.
Days are specified for the waxing moon. The markings enclosed by parentheses are for the waning moon.

Part II

There is no pleasure on the earth
that can possibly match spiritual joy.
There is no joy like that which comes from wisdom.
For when a human being truly experiences
the pleasures which come from spirituality,
he or she no longer has a taste for anything else.

—Joseph Michael Levry (Gurunam)

Chapter Eleven

The Fall of Man

God existed before any created thing, before the world of nature, man, plant and animal. He encompassed every possibility. He existed without want, limitation, hindrance or insufficiency. For reason knowable to itself, God emanated from its own immensity, a class or group of spiritual beings. At the time of their emanation, they received laws of order and purpose appropriate to their natures and free will.

The first class of beings originally belonged to the angelic hierarchies. They were sent to the earth with a given mission. They were free to stay or return to where they had come from. They chose to stay, because they thought that they could do very well without the will of God. As a result of the rebellious angels refusing to return to the divine source and cutting themselves from God, they became the fallen angels, known as the lords of darkness. They retained all their science and knowledge, but they lost the most important thing: they lost contact with Divine love and became creatures of evil. They formed an egregore, which is a symbol of the serpent coiled around the Tree of Knowledge of Good and Evil. The Tree itself is a symbol of the two currents of light and darkness, the former flowing from above, which stands for heaven or the Sun, and the latter ascending from below, which represents hell or Earth. Their crime was that they turned their will against God. They willed to change the order and purpose of their beings and even desired to challenge the powers of the creator by creating other beings themselves—something that was absolutely forbidden to them. God then punished them by absenting itself from them and thrusting them into the prison house of the material world. Therefore, God emanated the material world to punish and teach them humility, obedience and harmonious cooperation.

God emanated a second group of spiritual beings known as Man-Gods, who were to be rulers of nature—the material creation—and the first perverse beings. This second group, called Adam, the collective Man, known in Kabbalah as *Adam Kadmon*, enjoyed enormous power and privileges. He had both free access to the center of the Universe and to the divine thoughts. He was clothed in a spiritual form of glory not subject to the ravages of time or the limitations of space. Here the collective Man refers to both Adam and Eve.

God first put Adam and Eve into the Garden of Eden in paradise. Unlike the traditional story where there was mention of only one tree, there were actually two types of trees in that garden: the Tree of Life and the Tree of Knowledge of Good and Evil. Again, God gave laws of order and purpose to Adam and Eve, as well as free will. They were told to only eat the fruit of leaves of the Tree of Life. The forces on the Tree of Life were very balanced and in complete divine harmony. Eating the leaves of the Tree of Life cured all disease and disturbances, and eating its fruit bestowed immortality and eternal life.

One duty of Adam and Eve was to rule over the first perverse beings and see that their necessary lesson was learned. In addition, Adam's particular task was to name and look for the animal belonging to the same region as the Human-Gods. Eve's task was to study and learn the properties of vegetation. Therefore, her job was to study the specific properties of plants. It was her exploration of the plants in the Garden of Eden that led her to the discovery of the other Tree. Because of her curiosity, she started to spend time looking at it and studying the forces that rise from below the Tree. Her curiosity of finding out about the forbidden tree moved her from the inspiration, delight and light of paradise to the depths of matter in the dark world. As a result, she became acquainted with the dark lords, or fallen angels, that had cut themselves off from God. Those acquaintances created a relationship of exchange. Since one becomes what one observes, she created a relationship of exchange with the forbidden Tree. Instead of exchanging energy with the Tree of Life fed from heaven, she began to exchange with the Tree of Knowledge fed from hell. The exchange with the forbidden Tree of Knowledge of Good and Evil led her to connect with the serpent, Shamael, the Prince of the fallen angels. The serpent enticed Eve to challenge the immutable and Absolute power of the Creator by tasting the fruit of the Tree of Knowledge of Good and Evil.

Eve, excited about her new discovery, could not wait to share her experience with Adam and induced him to do the same. Adam approached the Tree and connected with Lilith, the female counterpart of the fallen angel Shamael. Filled with pride and willfulness, Adam and Eve succumbed to these temptations and attempted spiritual operations beyond their ordained powers. They set their will against the immutable will and decrees of God, and thus sinned by tasting the fruits and leaves of the forbidden Tree of Knowledge of Good and Evil. This is how Adam and Eve committed the 'original sin.' As a result of Adam and Eve's weakness and inability to resist temptation, and their misuse of free will, they were possessed by the corrosive forces which gradually solidified their bodies. This created a separation from the land of light in which they had dwelt.

This is how we, humanity, lost our body of spiritual form clothed in glory. We were forced to exchange our glorious form for a material body that was subject to the action of time, space and created beings. Therefore, we started to live in spiritual darkness, privation, pain, sorrow and misery.

By falling, Adam and Eve stopped dwelling in the center of the divine thought in the land of light. Since our collective 'banishment' to the denser world of matter, there have been ceaseless struggles to overcome the limitation and suffering imposed by the Fall in order to obtain reconciliation with the Creator and recover the lost status of Human-God—the favored and intimate one of the eternal power. There has been the hope and longing of the human race to return, but no one can find true happiness until the collectivity of humankind has completely regained divine favor and obtained oneness, absorption and reintegration with the creator of all.

Adam is the masculine principle and Eve is the feminine principle. Adam dwells in Tiphareth (the Sun) and Eve dwells in Yesod (the Moon). Adam, or Tiphareth, is closer to God (Kether), whereas Eve, or Yesod, is closer to Malkuth, the region of the Earth that stands right above the region of the Kliphoth—the unbalanced, chaotic forces symbolized in the bible story of the serpent. The Kliphoth are the dark side of the Sephiroth. It is from this dark world that the serpent climbed up into the Tree and succeeded in seducing Eve. Eve, or Yesod, is the foundation of the whole Tree of Life. She is the balance and stability of the whole edifice. If Eve, or Yesod, was attached to Adam, or Tiphareth, it would have maintained equilibrium of the edifice, because Adam was anchored to Kether (God). By allowing herself to be seduced by the serpent, she turned her attention downward and ceased to support the harmony of the whole edifice. As a result, Adam's attention went in the same direction and the whole edifice crumbled because they lost their balance. Thus, they were banished to the dark world of the Kliphoth.

❀

The story of Adam and Eve is a parable full of symbolism. The same story is constantly replayed to every man and woman who cut themselves off from their divine essence. Obviously, one can not cut themselves off from that which created them and breathes through them, but one can deny the existence of their divine connection, and in turn are thrown into illusory darkness. The link to God is the secret of life; it keeps the edifice together.

Adam prefigures creation. Eve is the facility of will or desire. Temptation is the initial impulse which sets the force of attraction and repulsion into motion. According to this account, it is the interplay of the will or the desire between the positive and negative aspect of forces that moves people through the world of their experiences.

In order to be holy, healthy and happy, the masculine and feminine principles must be dedicated to a divine cause. The goal of all *Hmm...*
spiritual science is to help one rebuild the spiritual body, which can
be used to return to the world of Light, called paradise. If we want
to return to the land of light from which we were expelled, we must
rebuild our spiritual bodies that we had when we still dwelled in that
Garden of Eden. At the time, the whole of nature obeyed us and the
animals neither feared nor harmed us. All creatures held us in
respect because of the light that shined from our face and entire
body. By losing that light, we lost our power over nature.

The tradition of the Fall of Man and his redemption and return
to the bosom of the Father is expressed by all religions. The Fall
brought us much closer to the region inhabited by the spirits that
had originally rebelled against divine authority. This is why it is easy
today to make contact with those spirits of darkness and for them
to plague us. It is much more difficult to get in touch with our
friends in the heavenly spheres because they are so much further
away. They are not far in physical distance, but in consciousness. By
praying and asking the spirit of light to help us, we get closer to
them. This connection may be difficult to maintain until the earth
gets cleansed and purified from the lurking forces of the Kliphoth,
who are constantly challenging and enticing us, especially through
the vices of the three lower chakras. For example, in the navel, they
manifest as power seeking, control, greed, egotism and anger; in the
sexual chakra, they manifest as fear, jealousy, revenge and lust with
its devastating effects on the soul; and in the rectum as instability,
insecurity and possessiveness.

We need more servants of the Divine so that the powerful light
of God may be released on the whole Universe. That light will eat
and absorb all darkness lurking in the air, water, soil, rocks and
plants. The increase in the number of children of light will remove
all the conditions and opportunities for evil intentions to manifest.

Therefore, by meditating on the Sun, we are contributing to
bringing in this glorious future of humankind, of heaven on earth.

We are creating the condition necessary for the manifestation of the children of God.

The serpent has neither hands nor feet, and according to universal symbolism, the feet and hands respectively stand for kindness and justice. The serpent represents our negative ego. It is our negative ego which caused us to move from paradise—the world of divinity, to the earth—the world of pain, disease, suffering and death, all of which belong to the world of duality. We need to work with light energy that comes from the Sun, and not the dark energy that comes from below the earth. Evil, or negativity, cannot enter the heart, for the heart is ruled by the world of divinity. It can only enter through our intellect, because it is ruled by the world of duality. Negativity insulates itself in a person's intellect. We tend to give more importance to the intellect than the heart. The intellect serves the ego, whereas the heart serves the soul. Those people who are not motivated by kindness, generosity and compassion use the intellect as a powerful tool to become rich and powerful, and to destroy their rivals. In other words, the intellect serves their personal interest. What we all must remember is that the intellect is here to serve the heart, not the ego. It is our sole preference of one and disregard of the other that causes severe imbalances.

The dark lords are highly intelligent, but they lack love. They use their intelligence to induce us to develop our intellect and stay away from the Heart, which is God. The intellect is given priority by those who are mainly interested in succeeding on the material plane, because they want to acquire power, glory, possessions and money. They behave like the fallen angels. They are not interested in building their spiritual body or communing with the Divine.

Chapter Twelve

Creation of the Universe

From the tradition of Kabbalah, the creation of the Universe can be easily described with the 22 letters of the Hebrew alphabet. These letters not only correspond to the 22 major arcana of the tarot cards, but also symbolize the 22 various levels of cosmic consciousness. Twenty-two is the number of longing and mastery of the mental realm. A very important Kabbalah book, called the Zepher Ietzirah, divides these 22 letters into 3 mother letters, 7 double letters, and 12 simple letters, thus forming the powerful 3–7–12 pattern of creation.

The whole Universe was proceeded by *emanation*. Emanation started with the spirit of God, which is the Word. This was the first step in creation. From the spirit of God emanated primordial air, which was the second step. From primordial air emanated primordial water, the third step, thus forming darkness and emptiness. From primordial water emanated the fourth step, primordial fire, whereby God established the throne of His glory. Out of these 3 elements of air, water and fire, He made His habitation.

Then He bound them with spirit and sealed them in the 6 directions: Above, Below, North, South, East and West. The 4 steps of creation, plus the 6 directions in space, creates the decade. This is called the *Decade out of Nothing*. Then the creation of the Universe followed.

All creation is played between time and space. First came the creation of space. Primordial fire developed itself into the visible Heaven. Primordial water condensed to form the seas and the lands of the Earth. Primordial air developed into the terrestrial atmosphere. Then came the cycle of time, in which fire developed itself into hot weather, water created cold weather, and air turned into moisture. Finally, primordial fire formed the head of the human body, primordial air formed the chest, and primordial water formed the body.

Thus, God used the three primordial elements of air, water and fire, which correspond to the 3 mother letters of the Hebrew alphabet: Aleph, Mem, and Shin, to create space, time, and humankind.

The next stage is symbolized by the 7 double letters of the Hebrew alphabet. The 7 double letters represent the major antitheses or dualities of life, named *Beth, Gimel, Daleth, Kaph, Peh, Resh* and *Tau*. These are the oppositions symbolized, respectively, by life and death, peace and war, wisdom and foolishness, wealth and poverty, beauty and ugliness, fertility and sterility, and dominion and dependence.

From the 7 letters came the 7 creative planets in space (Sun, Moon, Mars, Mercury, Jupiter, Venus and Saturn), the 7 days of the week in time, and the 7 gates of kingdom in humanity (two eyes, two ears, two nostrils and one mouth).

The final step is represented by the 12 simple letters: *He, Lamed, Vau, Nun, Zayin, Samekh, Cheth, Ayin, Teth, Tzaddi, Yod* and *Qoph*. These 12 letters correspond to the 12 signs of the zodiac in space, or the Universe, and to the 12 months of the year in time. In humanity, they correspond to the hands, feet, kidneys, spleen, small intestines, colon, gall bladder and reproductive organs.

Thus, through the 22 letters and 10 numbers, it took 32 mysterious steps to create the world, time and humanity.

Lifting the Veil mainly focuses on the central aspect of the creation pattern symbolized by 7, a number of divine power.

The Ten Spheres

For one to be skilled in divine work, one must have pure intentions. One must first understand that there is one and only one great cause. From that cause emanates other causes, such as Archangels and angels. God, the great cause, operates through 10 divine names. Those 10 divine names are different aspects of God. They are represented by the 10 spheres that make up the Tree of Life. In the following explanation, it will help to remember that Air = Movement; Water = Concentration; and Fire = Expansion.

No. I is Kether, or *Neptune*

The first sphere is the crown. It is the fountain of life. This 'Supreme Crown' of God represents the first impulse in 'EN SOPH, which sets in motion the process of becoming revealed. It is no more than a kind of movement in 'En Soph, the emergence of a will in that which is beyond willing. This is not, as yet, the will to create, but a will to will. It is also the door, the 'curtain' mentioned before, through which 'En Soph will act on the other Sephiroth. From this is produced the *will to create*, known as Hokmah.

Neptune acts like a superior form of Mercury. It is the air aspect of Air, which stands for the mobility of movement. This sphere is commonly called the *macroprosopus*. This is God, the burning force of the bible, or the house of the holy living creatures, often called *chayoth haqadesh*. The name Kether is often called *Merkabah*, which signifies the chariot.

Metatron, who is the prince of all the angels, is also the prince of the angels serving under Kether. Angels who serve under this sphere are called *Seraphim*, of which there are eight. The power of Metatron governs the months.

The essence of Kether is the will and the creative force, for without it nothing gets done. The will precedes every power. It is the power of realization. Without will, a man is one of the living dead.

No. 2 is Hokmah, or *Uranus*

Hokmah (or Chokmah) is the Wisdom, *Absolute Wisdom*. It is the upwelling spirit of Kether in positive action, the power house of the Universe. The primordial Male is called ABBA, Father.

This is the wheel of the zodiac. It is the Father, whose divine name is *Yah*, and its Archangel is Ratziel. Ratziel is the prince of the cherubim, of which there are eight. This is the house of Providential assistance, universal love and wisdom. Ratziel turns negativity into positivity.

Hokmah stands for Uranus, which is a superior form of Venus. This is the water aspect of Air—contraction checks movement. In other words, when Uranus is on you, it slows down your progress, making movement difficult. Since movement is life, water contracts the life.

No. 3 is Binah, or *Saturn*

Binah is the Intelligence of God, *Absolute Understanding*, where the details of all created things are actualized in Divine Thought. The primordial Female is called AIMA, the Mother.

These three Sephiroth make up the Supernals, The Upper Holy Trinity. This is the most important of the three triadic divisions of the Sephiroth, for it symbolizes the dynamic function of a thought process anterior to the world, and therefore an archetypal model. It represents, in other words, the thought process of God.

This is the house of the holy spirit, or *Shekinah*. Its divine name is *YHVH Elohim*, with its Archangel Tzaphkiel. This is the Mother, the Shakti energy, Mary—the mother of Jesus. It is the pure light. Tzaphkiel is the prince of the angels serving under Binah, called the *Trones*.

Saturn is the teacher who gives you the capacity to think and understand. It is fire of Air. Fire is expansion of movement, which creates space for learning and wisdom. Saturn operates through two signs. First, through Capricorn, it gives us what we need to live with others in society. Second, Aquarius brings us knowledge of cosmic laws and how to use them.

No. 4 is Chesed (or Hesed), or *Jupiter*

Chesed is the Mercy, the *Love of God*, i.e., the flow of divine grace through which the creation is effected. But this grace is too rich and prolific on its own; its superabundance must be controlled and confined if finite creatures are to exist. The Divine Light must be screened from view if it is to be endured. This limitation is brought about by the fifth Sephirah: Geburah.

In Hebrew, Chesed means mercy. This is the house of Dharma. Jupiter, who is the lord of wellness, stands for abundance, authority and generosity. Jupiter is water of Fire. It is the contraction aspect of expansion. From the expansion of movement comes the contraction of the expansion to bring the mercy.

The divine name of God in the house of Jupiter is *El*. The Archangel of this house is Tzadkiel, who is the prince of the eight dominations. The divine power of God manifests through Jupiter. Jupiter expresses itself through two astrological signs. Via Sagittarius, Jupiter gives us our spirituality. Through Pisces, Jupiter creates the outward expression of human feelings. Zeus is the Greek name for Jupiter. Zeus has power over lightning and storms. *Gedulah*, which is another name for Jupiter, means majesty and greatness. Jupiter bestows material and spiritual wealth.

No. 5 is Geburah, or *Mars*

Geburah, which is also known as Gevurah, the Justice or Strength, the *Power of God*, is chiefly manifested as the power of stern judgment and punishment. Power is the source of divine justice and control. The Sephiroth of Mercy (4) and Power/Justice complement each other. Power limits the abundance of Mercy; Mercy tempers the severities of Power.

This is the house of power and energy. The divine name of God in this house is *Elohim Gibor*, meaning God of might. The Archangel of this house is Kamael, who is responsible for the eight powers.

Mars is the planet of the God of war; it is the planet of warriors and justice. The energy of Mars brings determination. It is fire of Fire, meaning expansion of expansion. Too much fire makes the energy of justice fiery, which means you get as much as you deserve. Mars functions through the astrological signs of Aries and Scorpio. Through Aries, it brings us face to face with our ego. Through Scorpio, it gives an awareness of self-love. The fusion of Mercy and Power results in:

No. 6 is Tiphareth, or the *Sun*

Tiphareth is the Beauty, the *love of God*, to which falls the task of mediating between the two preceding Sephiroth. Beauty is the source of all beauty here below, for beauty consists of the harmonious balance between stark severity and sweet sentimentality. In Kabbalist thought the Divine Power is necessary for creation. It is only when man by his deeds disturbs the balance among the Sephiroth (for, as we have already seen, his life mirrors the world of the Sephiroth and *he can influence them*) that the quality of Power becomes isolated and results in the existence of evil.

This is the house of beauty and harmony. The divine name of God in this house is *YHVH Eloa Va Daath*, meaning the lord God of knowledge. Its Archangel is Raphael, the healing power of God. Raphael is the prince of the eight virtues. Christ, Ra, Apollo, Dionysis, and Krishna reveal a lot about this house. It is a sphere of balance. It expresses itself through the astrological sign of Leo, both forming our consciousness and giving us transcendence of personality. It is air of Fire. The movement aspect of expansion brings you beauty of light.

No. 7 is Netzach, or *Venus*

This is Victory. It is at the base of the Pillar of Mercy, and represents the creative imagination. This is a sphere of glory and victory. The divine name of God in this house is *YHVH Tzevaot*, the lord God of hosts. Its Archangel is Haniel, who is the prince of the eight principalities.

Venus is water of Water. After expansion of movement comes the contraction of contraction to bring the victory and pleasure. Venus rules Libra and Taurus. Through Libra, Venus merges our masculine and feminine sides. Through Taurus, Venus gives us awareness of beauty in the material world and love of physical beauty.

This house represents the fire of emotions and feelings, without which no creation is possible. Victory leads to ecstasy, pleasure, love, art, beauty and fulfillment, which are the realms of Venus. It is here that you receive devotion and love. It provides us with the qualities of desire and lust, as well as kindness, magnetism and charm.

No. 8 is Hod, or *Mercury*

This sphere is Splendor. It is at the base of the Pillar of Severity, and represents the image making concrete mentation of the mind—all that is usually meant by "mentality." In a properly balanced person, the two factors of NETZACH and HOD should be equilibrated. If a person has too much Netzach and too little Hod, you will have a highly imaginative but impractical so-called "arty" type. If there is too much Hod and little Netzach, you have the dry-as-dust academician. The result of the combination of these two Sephiroth manifests itself in Tiphareth as the philosophical or religious attitude of the person: in Yesod as your instinctual behavior, and in Malkuth as your physical being and affairs of the world.

This is the house of mental and intellectual capacities. It is here that you find eloquence, as well as mental fluctuation. The divine name of God in this house is *Elohim Tzevaot,* and its Archangel is Michael, the prince of the Archangels.

Mercury expresses itself through two astrological signs. Through Gemini, it brings out our thoughts. Through Virgo, it moves us from material possession to spirituality. Mercury is the planet of Hermes, the God of commerce, wealth and good fortune. Mercury is fire of Water.

No. 9 is Yesod, or the *Moon*

Yesod is the Foundation, the basis, the source of all active forces in God. Beauty also pours its forces into Foundation, so that this Sephirah conveys the flow of all the Sephiroth into the tenth Sephirah.

This is the house of the lunar God. It is the sphere of fertility. Its quality is foundation. The divine name of God in this house is *Shaddai El Chai,* meaning almighty living God, the lord of generation. Its Archangel is Gabriel, who is responsible for the eight angels called *Ishim.*

The Moon rules the astrological sign Cancer. It is air of Water, the movement aspect of contraction, which creates the foundation. Richness comes from condensing expansion and movement of the present. Through Cancer, the Moon gives us awareness of our emotional personality.

This is the house of imagination and memory. It is here that you will find the generative power of nature. This force coordinates and harmonizes everything. The chemistry of the solar system, the earth, and our bodies are stimulated by this force. It is called the astral world, whose projection is the material or objective world. The only way to affect anything in the material plane is to first change it in the astral plane.

No. 10 is Malkuth, or *Earth*

Malkuth is the Sovereignty, the *Kingdom of God,* from which the divine grace is diffused into the lower worlds to enable them to exist. It thus represents the creative principle at work in the finite world.

This is the kingdom. The divine name of God on Earth is *Adonoy Ha Aretz,* God of the Earth. Its Archangel is Sandalphon, the prince ambassador of the Earth, who is responsible for the *Kerubim*—the rulers of the elements. For the success of any operation, calling on Sandalphon may be extremely helpful.

The Tree of Life and the Four Worlds

Kether, which is our ego/will, is necessary for any manifestation. Without the will, there is no manifestation. The will needs the four worlds for material crystallization. Those four worlds are the mental, astral, etheric and physical worlds.

The Tree of Life can be divided into three triangles. The first triangle corresponds to the mental world. In this particular triangle, the third point is Daath, as opposed to Kether. Kether, in this particular case, is excluded. In this triangle, Chokmah is the realm of abstract thought, whereas Binah is the realm of concrete thought. They are both balanced by Daath, the realm of intellect. By working with Daath, we have the power to control and balance abstract and concrete thoughts. Daath controls the world of thought. Daath is also the borderline between the world of thought and the astral world. In other words, we can also control the astral world by working with Daath. Daath is called the fountain of knowledge; it is the door to the akashic records.

The middle triangle of the Tree of Life symbolizes the astral world. Chesed is the realm of superior or positive desires, whereas Geburah is the realm of passions or negative desires. They are both balanced by Tiphareth, which is the realm of desire with consideration of others' well-being, or healthy desire which benefits all. By working with Tiphareth, we can redirect our desires in a healthy manner to elevate all. Tiphareth is right above the etheric world, which is the world of formation. We can control the etheric world by working with Tiphareth.

The third triangle symbolizes the etheric world. Netzach (Venus) corresponds to the *light ether*, which is necessary for the activity of our senses and feelings, whereas Hod (Mercury) is responsible for the *reflecting ether*, which nourishes our thinking activity and takes care of our memory. Yesod (the Moon) is responsible for the *vital*, or *life ether*, necessary for vivification of the material body and reproduction. Also, Yesod is responsible for the *chemical ether* necessary for maintenance of the material body, such as assimilation and growth. Yesod is right above the physical world, Malkuth. Working with Yesod will allow you to control the material world. Malkuth is responsible for gases, such as oxygen for breathing; liquids, such as blood for circulation; and solids, such as the bones.

Let's explain the Tree from Malkuth to Kether. Malkuth is the Tree and Kether is the seed. Malkuth is the lowest level and Kether is the highest. You cannot experience the highest level unless you experience the lowest level. Kether is the will required to start an action; Malkuth is the result. Kether is the sequence; Malkuth is the consequence. We must know the Malkuth, or consequence, of the Kether, or sequence, we are about to start. Always know the Malkuth and you will be able to control the quality of Kether. Malkuth is Earth, which includes humanity. It is the world of elemental forces governed by the five *tattvas*: ether, air, fire, water, and Earth. There is no Kether without Malkuth, and no Malkuth without Kether. The person who cannot see the orange tree in its seed (Kether) cannot see God in this world.

All great Kabbalists know that the last lines to the Pater Noster are pure Kabbalah. That involves Malkuth and the lower triangle made up of:

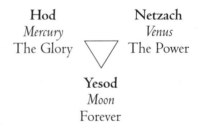

Hod   **Netzach**
Mercury   *Venus*
The Glory   The Power

Yesod
Moon
Forever

This is the Kingdom/Malkuth/Earth. What does it mean? It means that control of the emotions gives power, and control of the mind gives glory. By balancing the mind with the emotions, one balances the astral light (Moon) forever. Control of the emotions stops impulsive behavior, and control of the mind renders one very positive. The Moon is, as well, the seat of instincts and the autonomic nervous system, which is associated with the viscera and inner center of the brain. It is responsible for the health of the body and mind.

The middle triangle is made up of Tiphareth, Geburah and Chesed. This triangle symbolizes the activity of God in the world. Chesed stands for the (G) generating principle; Tiphareth is the (O) organizing principle; and Geburah is the (D) destroying principle. Chesed (Jupiter) and Geburah (Mars) symbolize the ups and downs of life. Tiphareth is the balance point. It is the center of higher consciousness, the central focus of the higher self. The lower self, or four lower Sephiroth, lasts only one human lifetime, whereas the higher self lasts for a whole evolution. Tiphareth is the seat of conscious and religious instinct. The great mystics call it "the point of the best in us."

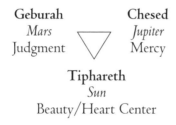

Geburah   **Chesed**
Mars   *Jupiter*
Judgment   Mercy

Tiphareth
Sun
Beauty/Heart Center

Then comes Daath, the abyss.

The upper holy trinity or triangle is made up of:

Kether
The Fountain of Light

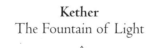

Binah   **Chokmah**
Intelligence   *Light/Love*
The Mother   The Father
Shakti

The mother-energy symbolizes the magnetic energy; the father-energy is the electric energy; and the light of Kether is the fountain of light. Kether, the crown, always shines through a balanced and strong electromagnetic field. As a result, one can safely walk through the oppositions of life, completely protected by a strong perception, resulting from a balance of both the mind and emotions. This makes one's stay in the kingdom of Earth very graceful, pleasant and happy. This is possible through the power of Naad, the word of God, through which the first spark of light, Kether, came to be.

Chapter Thirteen

The Star of David

The Kabbalah six-pointed star, commonly called the Star of David, can be used to improve your health or invite the beneficial influences of nature into your life. The six-pointed star is made up of two interlaced triangles. The triangle whose apex points up stands for the solar or electric force, whereas the triangle whose apex points down represents the lunar or magnetic force. Thus, the Star of David is a perfect expression of the basic principle governing life: electricity and magnetism. In other words, life, which is a vibration —meaning up and down—is the result of electric and magnetic forces. These two principles rule everything.

The Star of David symbolizes that which is known as the spiritual wedding or *Mysterium Conjunctionis* of the Alchemists. The coming together of the upper heaven triangle with the lower earth triangle produces spiritual gold, allowing blessings to fill one's life.

This is the true spiritual marriage born from the union of spirit and matter, heaven and earth, or the masculine and feminine principles. It is the merging of the male and female principles to bring about a condition of manifestation. The source of spirit is above, whereas the origin of matter is below. In the same way, the divine spiritual wisdom like spirit, comes from above, and the intellect, originates from below. Thus, the upper triangle with the apex down represents spirit or the divine spiritual wisdom. The lower triangle with the apex up stands for matter or the intellect. When we neglect our spirit, and only focus on the lower triangle, symbolized by money, power, sex or the material world, we cut ourselves from heaven, and create an imbalance within ourselves, which affects our health and peace of mind.

When we allow spirit to come down into matter in order to spiritualize it and make it alive, we see the light of the soul. Connecting with the soul brings the harmony of heaven in our life. In truth, matter needs spirit because in itself, it has no life. It is dense and opaque. It is spirit that makes it transparent and bright, alive and expressive, refined and godly. With the descent of spirit into matter, we allow the body to become a perfect temple for the holy ghost, leading to health, wholeness and harmony.

The heart and intellect are also expressed by the Star. The upper triangle stands for our heart, intuition or Eve, whereas the lower triangle represents intellect, logic or Adam. By working with the sacred science, we merge the wisdom of the heart with the intellect and enable truth to declare itself to us, through us, and as us. The union of both triangles not only gives intuitional logic, but it also confers a state of consciousness that is a state of grace and divinity.

The Star of David is also applicable to spiritual and material richness. Material richness corresponds to the earth or fire triangle of the Star of David with the apex pointing up. Very often, wealth without spiritual wisdom is a curse; it releases the unfettered and dangerous energies of the inferior astral world which progressively attract upon one the destructive forces of nature. It causes the fire of sex, money and power to progressively eat one alive. It takes away peace of mind and affects one's mental, emotional and physical health. One needs spiritual richness symbolized by the heavenly or water triangle, in order to balance the energy of money. Wealth along with spiritual wisdom is a blessing. It creates in a person's life the perfect manifestation of the Star of David, bestowing upon one, divine grace and peace.

Man is also like a living Star of David. The human body has an electro-magnetic field called the aura, which is composed of an electric and magnetic principle. Unhappiness, physical pain, discomfort and disease come from an imbalance in these two principles. Therefore, since the Star of David is a perfect expression of balance of the electric and magnetic principles, all we have to do is visualize or wear the Star upon ourselves to invite healing, harmony and blessings into our lives. Most importantly, if a proficient Kabbalist works with your place and date of birth to determine exactly the precious or semiprecious gemstone(s) which embody the beneficial influences of your ruling planets, and such a stone is placed at the center of a piece of jewelry in the form of the two triangles, wearing such a star automatically nurtures and rebuilds your electro-magnetic force. It can awaken the life-force and heal by redirecting all the constructive forces of the body, so that health may be restored and adversity deflected. This is one of many other applications of the Star of David.

As aforementioned, the Star is made up of solar and lunar forces. The solar force is the fire element, and the lunar force is the water element. When the mind, body and spirit are out of balance, we are at the mercy of negative karmic patterns, which manifest as anger and fear. These two powerful emotions are not only responsible for numerous diseases, they also attract adversity upon us. It is a disturbance in our fire element which brings out anger, whereas a disturbance in the water element brings fear. Under both cases, we are at the mercy of negative fate, because we are not in control of our mind, body and spirit. As a result, our perception of the truth is clouded.

THE STAR OF DAVID

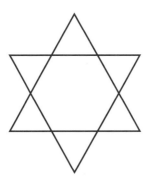

✿ EXERCISE TO HEAL IMBALANCES IN FIRE OR WATER

To heal an imbalance in the fire or water elements, follow this procedure.

1. Too much fire:
Since anger manifests as fire and heat, you need water to cool it off.

POSITION

Sit down in a comfortable, meditative position with the spine straight, hands on lap. If sitting in a chair, have the feet flat on the floor. If sitting on the floor, have the legs crossed.

PROCEDURE

Inhale deeply. Hold the breath for a few seconds. On the exhale, chant one long **MA** until you run out of breath. This sound invokes the water or Mother energy to nurture, calm and balance the fire of anger. Repeat this 7 times. Afterwards, sit quietly to allow the new energy to circulate and integrate.

2. Too much water:
In a state of fear we are completely frozen and cannot act. We need some warmth to keep the body going and energy to generate action. In the case of too much water, do the following:

POSITION
Same as above.

PROCEDURE

Inhale deeply. Hold the breath for a few seconds. On the exhale, chant one long **RA** until you run out of breath. This sound invokes the fire or Father energy to bring energy, warmth and strength in times of fear. Repeat this 7 times. Afterwards, sit quietly to allow the new energy to circulate and integrate.

Creating the Energy of the Star of David: RAMA

Chanting RAMA has the power to merge the energy of the Sun and Moon and surround us with the beneficial influences of the Star of David.

There are five elements, and they are earth, water, fire, air, and ether. RAMA represents fire and water, and of these five elements, water and fire fluctuate the most.

Water, which corresponds with the second chakra, shows fluctuating and fleeting sexual desires. Every spiritual person is tested by sex, money, and power. Sex symbolizes the second chakra, and we all know the dire consequences of its abuse. Money and power can be symbolized by the fire element. An imbalance of fire, which corresponds to the navel or third chakra, shows how inconstant people can be. Many murders have been committed for the purpose of money, and many people have been led off the spiritual path in quest of money. In addition, the obsession with control of others is a result of an imbalance in the navel chakra.

This clearly displays the fluctuations that the sun and moon, symbolized by fire and water, can bring into one's life when they are not balanced. The Star of David represents these two forces, because out of the five elements, the balance of fire and water is vital.

Chanting RAMA steadies the fire and water elements and stabilizing the fluctuations of life. RAMA is a powerful protective mantra. It has been used by students of both Kundalini yoga and Kabbalah to strengthen the electro-magnetic field, thereby creating a protective field around the person who chants this mantra. Vibrating RAMA can generate protection and luck, and dispel negativity.

MEDITATION:
BALANCING SOLAR AND LUNAR ENERGIES

RAMA

RA is the Sun energy, the positive and generating force
A is to come into existence
MA is the Moon energy, the negative and receptive force

POSITION
1. Sit in Easy Pose with the spine straight.
2. The hands are resting on the knees in Gyan mudra, the tips of the thumb and index finger pressed together.
3. The eyes are focused at the point between the brows.

MANTRA
First take a few deep breaths to calm the mind. Then, inhale deeply, and on the exhale, chant beautifully and rhythmically:

Rrraaaaa Mmmaaaaa

The tone is sonorous and soothing. Each repetition of RA-A MA-A should take about four seconds. Take the breath as needed.

COMMENTS
RAMA used to be one of the most widely practiced mantras, because it works. It belongs to those who practice it. We have an instinct to refine and condense or round off. In perception studies, we've seen that people will put a set of objects into patterns, even if it means excluding, or not even seeing, one object outside the pattern. Humankind has always created secrets to insure that the knowledge we had was not rounded off and lost. In various secret groups, there were rituals and codes of initiation. These evolved to insure that people in the group were on the same frequency of communication.

Anyone not on the same frequency cannot understand another person without losing or misinterpreting part of the communication. A secret makes it personal. We become personal and secret because we are afraid to be misunderstood. Man has two instincts: to be social and communicate, and to round off and condense. These seem to be at odds. In reality, there is nothing that is secret or should be secret. There are no secret or personal mantras. These are humanity's creations, not Nature's. Unfortunately, the sound of RA-A MA-A that calls and merges the Sun and Moon energies, got condensed to RAMA and even to RMA.

Yogi Bhajan described this need for common frequency in communication this way: "...Understanding is only in relationship to the frequency of the level of communication and receiving."

Chant RA-A MA-A without abbreviation and without secrecy. Communicate and share. Chanting in a group will bring you to the same frequency of communication with each other, and will expand your intuition to understand one another.

Metals

The great African mystics understood the importance of the fire and water, sun and moon, and the need to balance these two energies in order to appease the fluctuations of life. They also knew the power of metals. They came up with a method that works tremendously to help balance the energies of the Sun and Moon.

These mystics knew that gold and silver respectively stand for the Sun and the Moon. They fused gold onto silver to steady the forces of life and make one more fortunate. Therefore, they would take a silver ring or bracelet and add a gold point on it.

This mixture of silver and gold can be a very powerful talisman, because it opens one to the beneficial influences of the Sun and the Moon. Wearing a ring made of gold and silver has the same effect as chanting RAMA, for these metals embody the vibrations contained in this mantra. Gold can be symbolized by RA, the Sun, and the masculine principle. Silver can be symbolized by MA, the Moon, and the feminine principle. Wearing a mixture of these metals can balance the two oppositional forces and increase one's luck.

Breath

The Pillar of Mercy symbolizes the male principle, or right nostril, whereas the Pillar of Severity stands for the female principle, or left nostril. God is in the middle pillar, the Pillar of Equilibrium. The middle pillar shows how vital breath is, for without breath, we are lifeless. Seventy-two hours before a person gets sick, there is a change in the breath rate. By having a daily love affair with the breath of life, it is possible to undercut most illnesses before they take over. The breath is our connection with God. In the mother's womb, the umbilical cord kept us nourished and alive. As soon as it is severed, the breath takes over.

SOLAR BREATH

The right nostril is symbolized by the Sun, which on the central pillar of the Tree of Life is Tiphareth. We know from Kundalini yoga that breathing from the right nostril stimulates solar energy in the body. When you have a lot of solar energy, you feel energetic, enthusiastic and extroverted. It stimulates heat in the body, so you will not feel cold. It also purifies the body and aids digestion. It is said that right-nostril breathing is good for those with a long-standing problem of low blood pressure. This type of breath is linked to the left side of the brain. Therefore, in order to have a clear, action-oriented, analytical mind, before starting any project, perform 26 long, deep breaths through the right nostril.

The mantra RA, which corresponds to the Sun, generates solar energies. RA contains the masculine principle and stimulates the left side of the brain. This mantra gives mental clarity as well. Chanting RA is equivalent to right nostril breathing.

LUNAR BREATH

The left nostril is symbolized on the central pillar of the Tree of Life by the Moon, or Yesod. It is linked to the solar plexus. Breathing through the left nostril is like getting a fresh supply of blood. It is said that left-nostril breathing also helps regulate high blood pressure. Those who suffer from insomnia should breathe through the left nostril in order to calm the mind and go to sleep, because it stimulates the cooling and calming functions of the body. I know from experience that anytime I suffer from insomnia, my left nostril is almost always clogged. What I will usually do is sleep on the right side of my body in order to unclog my left nostril. You can experiment for yourself. Whenever you cannot sleep, check which nostril is blocked. Most likely, it will be the left nostril.

Similar to chanting RA for solar energy, the mantra MA brings Moon energy into the body. MA stands for the feminine principle and stimulates the right brain. Chanting MA is similar to breathing through the left nostril. It calms the nerves and moves the energy from the brain down.

Throughout the day, our breathing switches every two and a half hours from predominantly the left nostril to the right nostril. The following simple exercise will help channel the breath from one nostril to the other.

TO OPEN THE LEFT NOSTRIL, TRY THIS EXERCISE

1. Place your left hand under your right armpit.
2. Bend the right arm at a 90° angle, make a fist, and press your upper arm against the side of your body.
3. Concentrate on breathing through the left nostril.
4. Do long, deep breathing for 3 minutes.

Note: The reverse can be applied to open the right nostril (place right hand under left armpit).

Developing one's spiritual nature is the most peace-giving
and inspiring practice which fills the heart
with true happiness and joy while improving one's health.
All other pleasures are not only temporary,
they also keep the heart restless and fill life with emptiness.
Whereas spiritual pleasure keeps the heart
full with the light of healing joy.
When a human invests in spiritual wisdom,
it takes such good care of him
that it transforms all misfortune into delight.

—Joseph Michael Levry (Gurunam)

Chapter Fourteen

Bringing in the Light

The Kabbalistic Cross

The Kabbalistic Cross is an effective formula, used by Kabbalists to create protection and stability in one's electro-magnetic field. Matter, or the lower self, must be purified so that a perfect environment may be created to allow the Spirit, or higher self, to fully incarnate in the body. Usually the holy Spirit will over-shadow most people until the purification of matter takes place. By performing the Kabbalistic Cross, we not only help in this purifica-tion process, but also, we invoke the assistance and guidance of our higher Self.

The vertical shaft of the Kabbalistic Cross corresponds to the fire element, or solar principle, whereas the horizontal shaft stands for the water element, or lunar principle. Among the five elements of ether, air, fire, water and earth, the solar and lunar principles fluctuate the most. It is the balance of fire and water that brings stability and harmony into our lives. The equilibrium created by this formula comes from the point located at the exact center of the cross, which is at the heart center, the reflection of the sun in us. It is the center of harmony, beauty and balance. Performing the Kabbalistic cross allows the harmony and balance of the heart center to permeate our entire aura.

The four branches of the cross refer to the four quarters of the globe—East, South, West and North, as well as the four elements of air, fire, water and earth. The Archangels Raphael, Michael, Gabriel and Auriel are, respectively, in charge of the East, South,

West and North quarters of space. Performing the Kabbalistic cross declares dominion of the spirit over the elemental forces.

The Kabbalistic Cross is a means of connecting with your light. It can be used before and after any spiritual work. It can also be used to restore balance and when you are in need of clarity.

PERFORMING THE KABBALISTIC CROSS

To perform the cross, face East (or in your mind's eye face symbolic East). See yourself standing so tall that your head touches the clouds. Visualize the psychic sun above your head. With the right hand, have the fingers in the Golden triangle (thumb, index, and middle fingertips together).

a. Touch the forehead and say *Atoh* (*Ah-toh*)
   (Thou art)
b. Touch the navel and say **Malkuth** (*Mal-kooth*)
   (the Kingdom)
c. Touch the right shoulder and say **Vegeburah** (*Vay-ghe-boo-rah*)
   (Power)
d. Touch the left shoulder and say **Vegedulah** (*Vay-ghe-doo-lah*)
   (Glory)
e. With your palms pressed together in prayer pose at the level
   of the heart, vibrate **Le...o...lam** (*Lay-oh-lahm*)
   (to the ages)
f. *A...me...n....*

As you say *Atoh*, see the light flowing from the sun into your body down to your feet. When you say **Vegeburah, Vegedulah**, see a band of light crossing you horizontally. The idea is to put yourself into a cross of light. When you bring your hands together and say **Le...o...lam**, visualize a beautiful pink light at the center of that cross of white light.

To Harmonize Your Energies With The Universe

1. Perform Kabbalistic Cross facing East.

2. Proceed with your right forefinger to draw a blue-flamed circle in a clockwise direction around you. The circle should be about 3 feet in radius. Return to the beginning position to close the circle.

3. Visualize the circle while you repeat the Kabbalistic Cross.

Hebrew and Gnostic Kabbalah Sacred Sounds

RUACH ELOHIM

To have a relationship with God, we must have a relationship with our soul. To know God, we must connect with our spirit. To experience super-consciousness in consciousness, the soul must be activated. Once this is done, the soul takes control of the body and its energies, thereby bestowing spiritual powers upon us, then everything starts working for us. The process of invoking our soul, so that it may take over and guide us, is called *the descent of the Holy Spirit into matter.*

There are certain words or combination of words, such as the Hebrew words *Ruach Elohim*, which have proven to be extremely effective in the soul awakening.

What is Ruach? In the beginning verses of Genesis, you will find the Hebrew words Ruach Elohim. Regarding the Gematria of Ruach: Resh, Vau and Cheth, respectively, gives 200, 6 and 8, resulting in the total of 214. In the Gematria of Elohim: Aleph, Lamed, Heh, Yod and Mem, respectively, give 1, 30, 5, 10 and 40, which when added together gives 86. When Ruach and Elohim are added (214 + 86), the result is 300, which also corresponds to *Shin.* Shin is the generative fire whose job is to facilitate the incarnation of the Holy Spirit into matter in order to spiritualize it. In other words, Shin is a symbol of spiritual birth. Therefore, Ruach Elohim, like Shin, by virtue of the same number, can activate the soul, thus filling us and our lives with the redemptive light of the Almighty.

The number 300 theosophically reduces to 3, which stands for the tarot card The Empress. The archetype of *the Empress* will bring harmony, beauty, fruitfulness and happiness into our lives.

Ruach signifies spirit and resides in the heart. It is active/passive. Ruach corresponds to Tiphareth on the Tree of Life. Tiphareth stands for the Sun and represents the heart center. It is also the seat of the will and rules the personality. Ruach is the second part of the soul to enter the body, which is with the first breath at birth, and it is the second aspect of the soul to leave the body at death. It exits through the mouth at the last breath.

The soul emanates from Adam Kadmon, the heavenly human. One's true essence is the soul, not the body. The body is just the flesh of the real person. Ruach is the root of outward consciousness, and allows one to become aware through forms and their expression. It is all conscious and unconscious mental activity. Everything that was ever made by humans has its beginning in Ruach. Ruach is the energy that gives rise to thoughts that will be brought into action.

PREPARATION

You must create absolute cleanliness and purity around you before invoking this pure Light. Therefore, shower before and remove all shoes or anything impure. Calling upon *Ruach Elohim* will give you the Light necessary to elevate your consciousness, so you may gracefully overcome the challenges of time and space. Therefore, direct that light for constructive purposes. Vibrate with absolute reverence.

HAND POSITION

Arms are relaxed at your side. Bend the elbows. The palms face up as to receive; they are neither directly in front of you or directly to the side, but in between. It is a very relaxed and natural position.

VISUALIZATION

Visualize a golden flame in your heart. Make it bright and intense. Let it reach out and enfold everyone and everything. Its effulgence spreads throughout the room, gaining in strength and brilliance. Let the light radiate out in all directions, expanding throughout the city. Radiating everywhere, envelop the nation, the continent, the world, and the whole Universe. You are one with the source of all light. There is nothing but light. You are light. Take a full, deep breath, then proceed to the next step.

SACRED SOUND

Take a deep breath and vibrate this sacred name of God **Ruach Elohim** *(pronounced roo-ach-ay-loh-heem)* as you exhale. Repeat 8 times.

Rrrooo-Aaach-Aaaay-Loooob-Heeeeemmmm

IAO

There is another Gnostic mantra, *IAO (pronounced ee-ah-oh)*, which has equal redemptive powers. *IAO* not only stands for Isis, Apophis and Osiris, but also has the capacity to activate the spirit within us. The Gematria of *IAO* gives us Yod (10), Aleph (1) and Vau (6), which adds up to 17, known as the *Star of the Magi*. It represents the eight-pointed star of Venus, which is the symbol of peace and love. When this vibration is properly activated, it will bring inspiration, radiance, clear vision and cosmic connection. It also represents the lifting of the veil and renewed vigor.

Meditation on the Line of Equilibrium

This exercise is known to bestow healing power upon the operator, also providing him/her with multiple blessings. It is an excellent preparation for visualization. This is one of the most powerful exercises known to Kabbalah.

THE MIDDLE PILLAR EXERCISE

1. Sit down or lie down on a firm surface. Relax.
2. Breathe deeply, slowly with rhythm.
3. Visualize a whirling sphere of approximately four inches in diameter, glowing with brilliant white light at the crown of the head.
   - Slowly vibrate the name of the sphere Kether: EHEIEH.
   - Inhale and chant the name on the exhale for a total of 8 cycles.
4. Visualize a column of light descending to form another sphere at the throat center, glowing with ultra-violet light.
   - Vibrate the name of JEHOVAH ELOHIM
     (*yeh-ho-vo eh-loh-heem*) for 8 cycles.
5. Visualize a column of light descending to form another sphere at the solar plexus, the color of clear pink rose.
   - Vibrate the name of the sphere Tiphareth: IAO or IESHOUAH (*yea-hesh-shoe-wah*). Do this 8 cycles.
6. Visualize light descending to form another sphere at the genital area, with a deep purple color.
   - Vibrate the name of the sphere Yesod: SHADDAI EL CHAI. Again 8 cycles.
7. Visualize light descending to the feet where they form another sphere of rich russet brown.
   - Vibrate the name of the sphere Malkuth: ADONOY HA ARETZ. 8 cycles.

8. Contemplate the middle pillar that you have established within yourself. Picture the five central Sephiroth as throbbing with energy on this middle pillar of brilliant light which connects them. Now, circulate the psycho-spiritual energy generated.

9. As you exhale, imagine the energy going down the left side of the body from the crown chakra to the feet. As you inhale, the energy travels up the right side from the feet to the head. Repeat this process 4 times.

10. As you exhale, imagine the energy pouring down the front side of the body from the head to the feet. As you inhale, imagine it rippling up the back of your body from the feet to the head. Repeat this process 4 times.

11. Now bring your attention to your feet. Imagine the energy rising up through the middle pillar to the crown of the head as you inhale. Then as you exhale, see it cascading down to the feet. Do it 4 times. This is the fountain exercise.

12. Now you can pray or make a wish.

BRINGING LIGHT INTO A SITUATION

1. THREE LONG, DEEP BREATHS

As soon as you feel like you are back in a dark area of life, you must remember that your mental life must work with one word. Therefore, think of *Light*. As you take a deep breath, hold the breath as you meditate on the words *Light of Light*, then exhale. Repeat this three times. The moment you think of Light, God prevails. Your energy changes, your projection becomes strong, and you cannot be defeated. By holding the breath, a chemical change is generated in your blood stream, rendering it more alkaline. As a result, the alkalization of the blood alters the chemical environment of the brain, thereby making you less impulsive and more centered. Why do we take three breaths? The number three was considered by the ancients to be a very sacred number. Even Aristotle, who was recognized as a great scientist, spoke highly of the number three. It symbolized the mystery of the trinity and stands for the triangle.

2. EXHALE SLOWLY TO THE COUNT OF 40

Focus all your attention on the exhale, making it slow and long, so as to reach the lower abdomen. This mode of breathing will keep you from getting both tired and emotionally unstable. This kind of breath is known to harmonize your consciousness with your environment. It strengthens the nervous system, balances the aura and makes you fearless.

3. BECOME CALM

Calmness fills the body with Light and brings clarity and centered-ness. Anytime that we are not calm, we lose energy and move away from the Light. By becoming calm, you allow the body to recharge itself and restore stability. Therefore, if you find yourself in a critical situation, and the above method is not enough, create a state of internal calmness.

4. BE IN THE PRESENT MOMENT

By being conscious of the breath, you connect with your spirit, while tuning into the present moment. Being in the here and now increases your light and awareness, thereby uniting your mind, body and spirit, to allow you to generate the right action. You are in touch with your spirit and guidance becomes automatic.

5. MEDITATE ON THE SUN

Meditate mentally on the light of the Sun. Those who relate to the light become light, and where there is light, you cannot find dark-ness. Meditating on the Sun creates harmony, balance and protection. It creates the condition for fulfillment and joy.

INVOKING THE LIGHT: LUMEN DE LUMINE

Lumen de Lumine symbolizes the ineffable presence of the supreme principle. Chanting or listening to *Lumen de Lumine* will create a communion between you and the beneficent and benevolent hosts of the superior astral world. It will connect you to the most powerful and protective egregore of the Rose+Croix Kabbalists. This mantra will provide physical protection against the ill will of other people. It is a prayer of the strongest potency, which will keep misfortune away and bring peace, love and mercy into the lives of those who chant or listen to it.

Lumen de Lumine is the only part recovered from the original Nicea Creed; the complete and original creed has been lost. The Nicene are the people who lived in the town of Nicaea near Constantinople, now known as Istanbul. Extensive use over the past 600 years by the Rose+Croix Kabbalists has empowered it on the collective psyche. As a result, it surrounds those who chant or listen to it with a blanket of light, and eats darkness from their lives. It opens the heart and brings serenity. It purifies and strengthens the aura. It will clear the energy in a room in a short time. Time has proven that holy blessings come to those who are in its company.

> LUMEN DE LUMINE
> DEUM DE DEO
> LUMEN DE LUMINE
> DEUM VERUM DE DEO VERO
> LUMEN DE LUMINE
>
> *(LIGHT OF LIGHT*
> *GOD OF GOD*
> *GOD BY THE WAY OF LIGHT*
> *LIGHT BY THE WAY OF GOD*
> *LIGHT OF LIGHT)*

A recording of this may be ordered through Rootlight, Inc. See the back of this book for more information.

Chapter Fifteen

Relationships
and the Law of the
Seven Creative Planets

There is a law known as the Law of the Seven Creative Planets. The matrix of change we call nature is structured by its forces. From the womb to the grave we are governed by its influences. Your day of birth sets this clock in motion, and every relationship dances with these planets as partners.

When to Enter a Relationship and How to Avoid Divorce

It is of absolute importance that you familiarize yourself with the impact of these Seven Creative Periods in your yearly cycle in order to become sensitive to the influence of these universal structures.

Our world is comprised of pairs. Therefore, life is engendered through the forces of vibration. This vibration of life presents itself in many ways. Day and night, good and evil are some of these ways. Within your own cycle's influence, these planets represent your "best" and "worst" time for specific accomplishments. For example, the Sun, Jupiter and Venus tend to be beneficent planets, whereas Mars and Saturn tend toward malignant aspects. The Moon and Mercury have a more neutral countenance.

Therefore, the best periods to enter into a relationship occur when you are in the cycle during the influence of the Sun, Jupiter or Venus. Those periods are extremely good for starting a relationship. Above all, starting a relationship during any of these periods while the Moon is waxing is excellent. By doing so you are giving the relationship every chance it needs to survive any trial.

Starting a relationship while the Moon is waning will not prove beneficent, as the waning Moon—which is the period from the full Moon to the day before the new Moon—is the best time to *remove* things from your life. Actually, it is the best time for divorce. One should *not* use the time dedicated to taking things *out* of one's life to bring *new* things in! By doing so, you increase the probability of disappointment and failure. Such a failure may be minimized by the impact of a more favorable period—it is your choice!

The sexual act, or bonding, determines the first day of the relationship. The clock of the seven planets is placed in motion with the bonding of a relationship. If the relationship makes it to marriage, the marriage date overrides the previous starting date. In other words, the marriage date becomes the new date for the impact of the influence of the seven creative planets.

The best time to enter a marriage is during your Sun, Jupiter and Venus period—especially when the Moon is waxing. Doing so will ensure that your married life will be more peaceful and harmonious. *Avoid entering a relationship during your Saturn and Mars periods!*

Saturn and Mars have a malignant focus, and the 52 days that each of these planets rule are accident-prone times of trial, during which you can make all types of mistakes that will resurface karmically later. Therefore, neither enter a relationship nor get married during those periods. An *especially* poor time is when the Moon is waning, as any relationship or marriage entered during this time will sooner or later experience serious complications and possibly end in painful divorce. However, if one enters a relationship in such a period and makes it to marriage, the negative energy can sometimes be deflected by setting the marriage date during your Sun, Jupiter or Venus period, especially while the Moon is waxing (the new Moon to the day before the full Moon). If you happened to have married during your Mars or Saturn periods and are undergoing marital problems, you can remarry during your best period to cool things down.

THE MOON AND MERCURY

During your Moon and Mercury periods, you can enter a relationship when the Moon is waxing. The Moon and Mercury periods, while the Moon is waning, are problematic, because during the waning Moon those two planets act like Mars and Saturn. Therefore, do not enter a relationship or marriage at that time.

Facing Challenges in a Relationship

The understanding and application of the seven creative planets can become a source of infinite wisdom.

As mentioned earlier, your personal year begins with your day of birth and continues to the day before your next birthday. The seven creative planets—Sun, Moon, Mars, Mercury, Jupiter, Venus and Saturn—have a direct impact on your yearly cycle. The first day of a relationship is determined by the first mutual act of sexual bonding. This is considered the "birthday" of the relationship, and like your personal cycle, it too follows the annual cycle influenced by the seven planets.

There are three challenging phases that an intimate couple must overcome for a relationship to last. For easy identification, they are called phases X, Y and Z.

PHASE X

Phase X lasts for about the first four months. The number 4 represents stability, base and foundation. It is a pair of pairs. It is "on the square." If the foundation is weak, the structure always collapses at the first trial.

The first 52 days which follow mutual bonding are governed by the Sun. This explains the intensity of passion, emotion, fun and excitement that couples usually experience in their beginning period.

Then come the next 52 days, ruled by the Moon period. The Moon signifies fluctuation. It either drives you apart or brings you closer together. In the first scenario, the Moon drives you apart and Mars *severs* the relationship. It is for this reason that some relationships end between the third and fourth months. In the second scenario, the Moon brings you closer and Mars *strengthens* the relationship, thus allowing it to go beyond the fourth month.

PHASE Y

There are some people whose relationship passes phase X, or month four, and stops before the end of the third year. This is the period we call Phase Y. The planets govern the relationship in a cycle of 7 years, from the Sun in year 1, to Saturn in year 7.

Sometimes a challenge is felt early in the eighth month, before the couple reaches the Saturn period of the first yearly cycle. Normally the second trial is within the second year, which is ruled by the Moon. If the relationship is not strong in the second year, it will never make it past the third year.

PHASE Z

I am sure you have heard of the "seven year itch," meaning that the seventh year is the most difficult in a marriage or intimate relationship. This is what can happen in Phase Z. Those who go beyond the third year are challenged in the sixth and seventh years. This is because the influence of Saturn can be felt as early as the sixth year, and comes into full effect in year 7 of the relationship. If the relationship continues past the seventh year, it has a good chance of lasting for a long time. Afterwards, you will be most challenged every 7 years.

No one can really engage with what they cannot see. Therefore, an understanding of these phases will help you recognize these challenges, and hopefully help you overcome them through your awareness of their influence on your relationships.

You can obtain extensive information on this subject in my book Alchemy of Love Relationships. *This book is vital for a healthy and successful love life.*

Chapter Sixteen

The Sun and the Four Seasons

As there are four important days in the lunar cycle, the yearly cycle of the Sun contains four powerful weeks. They are the weeks of:

March 18–24
June 18–24
September 18–24
December 18–24

Out of these weeks, the most powerful days of the year are:

Spring Equinox (March 21)
Summer Solstice (on or around June 21)
Autumn Equinox (on or around September 21)
Winter Solstice (on or around December 21)

During the equinoxes, the days and nights are equal because the Sun crosses the Earth's equator. During the solstices, the day is the longest in the summer, and shortest in the winter. The length of the day and amount of sunlight symbolize the activity in the body, for in summer, the body expands, and in winter, the body contracts. This can be demonstrated by the wearing of a ring. It will be looser in the winter and tighter in the summer. Again, you will be more active in the summer, because summer falls within the full period of Mars in the yearly cycle.

The equinoxes and solstices are important days because the Sun releases vast quantities of energy, which can be used to heal the mind, body and spirit. <u>These are the best days for both spiritual advancement and improvement of health.</u>

Spring

Spring, which extends from March 21 to June 20, is one of the most powerful healing and energized seasons of the year. It is a time for new beginnings. During these months, the Sun showers the Earth with more prana than at any other time of the year. One very striking peculiarity to be found in Spring is the abundance of green energy present in Nature. Such quantity of green is associated with an abundance of Sun energy. This can be demonstrated in the following way:

If you take a prism and filter the light of the Sun, you will see the seven colors of the spectrum. These colors correspond to the seven chakras, or nerve centers, along the spine. These nerve centers are a reflection of the seven positive centers of consciousness located in the brain. The seven nerve centers work through the spinal column, as the seven Archangels before the throne work through the seven creative planets.

Green, which is the center color, corresponds to the heart center. This in turn is a reflection of the Sun in us. That is why in Spring one cannot help but remark on the abundance of green energy. It is certainly worth using this time to <u>cleanse and rejuvenate the body</u>. In this connection, the body can be compared to a car driven by a chauffeur, which in this case is the soul. Many drivers know that, if your car receives years of neglect, it will probably break down and need costly repairs. As surely as servicing a car can prevent break-downs, so regular care of the body can prevent diseases. That is why the best time to service the physical body with the healing energy of prana is during the Spring. Regardless of how poor your health may have been until then, this is your chance to increase the amount of prana in the body and zap the illness out. The chief point to remember is that the more prana you have, the healthier you can be. In truth, diseases cannot remain in the presence of abundant prana.

Spring is symbolized by the index finger, which is ruled by the planet Jupiter. Jupiter represents expansion and material wellness.

One can use this energy to heal and renew. This season should be used for total rejuvenation and purification of the body. It is the best time to do a lot of breathing exercises and spend time walking or jogging outdoors.

REGARDING FOODS

A green diet will give you vitality and Sun energy. Eat a lot of green vegetables as well as fresh fruits. Vegetables will bring you subtle energies, whereas fruits will provide you with heavenly energy. In connection with this, lightly steamed vegetables are the best source of energy. Further, to help the cleansing process, squeeze the juice of half a lemon in a glass of warm water and drink. You may sweeten it with a touch of honey.

REGARDING EXERCISE

Do a lot of breathing exercises and walk as frequently as you can. Needless to say, breath is one of the best ways of bringing prana into the body. Walking, on the other hand, will work on your divine body. Your feet are your foundation. You should soak them in salted warm water. There is no part of the body that cannot be healed through the feet, and since they take you everywhere, give them special treatment.

HEALING BREATH MEDITATION

POSITION

Sit in a comfortable, meditative position, with your spine erect and your legs crossed, or with your feet flat on the floor if you are sitting in a chair. The eyes are 1/10th open, looking at the tip of your nose.

MUDRA

Your right thumb touches your right ring fingertip. Do the same with your left hand.

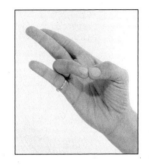

BREATH

Inhale to the count of 20.
Hold to the count of 20.
Exhale to the count of 20.

TIME

Continue for 11 minutes and build up to 31.

COMMENTS

This is an extremely powerful pranayam meditation. It will give you power over life and death. The ring finger represents the Sun. That finger channels the life force. By touching the thumb to the ring finger, you can attract nerve strength, health and vitality into your life.

Summer

The Summer Solstice is June 21. This is the second of the four most powerful days of the year. It is the longest day; therefore an abundance of light showers the Earth. Because there is more light during this season, it is an excellent time to dispel darkness and expand one's inner light.

Summer represents the ring finger, which is ruled by the Sun. The ring finger stands for health and nervous energy. One can use this period to strengthen the life force in the body.

If you look at the 7 cycles, Summer falls in the Moon and Mars periods. The Moon clearly indicates sexual energy. I am sure lots of people can attest to the influence of Summer as far as that department is concerned. Most lovers meet during this time. Mars indicates an abundance of physical energy. When we combine the influences of both planets, we can say that summer stimulates the use of sexual energy. In order to speed up our evolutionary development, we should focus on freeing up our angelic side, rather than getting caught up with the impulsive energy of this season.

Autumn

September 21 is the Autumn equinox, and it is the third-most powerful day of the year. Autumn stands for the pinkie, or Mercury, finger. It is ruled by Mercury and Jupiter in the yearly cycle. Needless to say, this is a restless period, so discrimination is required. Most students are back in school, and parents have to worry about paying the cost of tuition. Often there are the logistics in transporting the children to and from school. It is also a good time for writing books and letters.

Winter

Winter solstice falls on December 21. It is the fourth-most powerful day of the year. This day is symbolized by the middle finger, which is ruled by the planet Saturn. Saturn means balance and discipline. One should be very balanced in expenditures; moderation during the winter should be observed. It is time for introspection and regrouping of one's energy and resources. This is the Night before the Day.

Winter falls in the Venus and Saturn periods. Everyone, without exception, knows what the three months that follow December 21 are about. The first half of this season is usually spent having fun. It is the holiday season, filled with parties and reunions. People spend lavishly on gifts for others and themselves. It is difficult to save money during this time. As Venus indicates, it is a time for fun.

The second half of the season is usually quite hard. Most people are broke in this period, because of the money they spent during the Venus period. No one can ignore the impact of Saturn, demonstrated clearly by the ravage of the weather. It is a time for snow, sleet, rain, hurricanes and so forth, which usually keep people bound indoors.

A word of advice: Spend money wisely during the first half of winter. Second, focus on your spirituality and get to know yourself better. Use discipline, as symbolized by the Saturn finger.

Chapter Seventeen

Practical Application of Mantras

Words constantly create and recreate our lives. Mantras are sound currents that are used to direct and redirect energy in order to clear darkness and negativity. They are sacred words of power. You may be surprised that in *Lifting the Veil*, this book on Kabbalah, there are only a few Hebrew words of power. The others are all drawn from Kundalini yoga. This is not because I underestimate the Hebrew words of power—they are indeed powerful. With use, their power grows in you. One key element of the 22 letters of the Hebrew alphabet is visualizing them. Their potency comes mainly from the combination of visualizing the letters and directing the movement of astral light to create a desired effect. The same is true for Gurmukhi words of power used in Kundalini yoga, except that chanting them alone will give you results on the spot. All you have to do is merge with the sound current and the results will be automatic. You actually do not have to worry about visualization, but if you chose to do so, adding visualization will increase their potency. Gurmukhi means "mouth of the Guru." Reciting words in Gurmukhi is the science of working the hypothalamus in order to take care of the autonomic nervous system and shift your projection to invite grace and protection into your life. It will stimulate the nervous system and rewrite your destiny.

215

POSITION

All the following mantras can be done for 11–31 minutes with your hands in prayer pose (palms pressed together with 5–10 pounds of pressure at the level of your heart and thumbs touching the sternum) unless otherwise specified. When you bring your palms together at the center of your chest, which is the location of the mind nerve, with the eyes focused at the third eye or root of your nose, the individual consciousness automatically merges with the supreme consciousness. The right hand channels solar life-force energy of positive polarity, and the left hand channels lunar relaxing energy of negative polarity. When these two energies are brought into balance, you enter a neutral state of consciousness. When the hands are pressed against the mind nerve, energy is conducted from the central nervous system into the mind, thereby completing the energy circuit. This creates a quiet, balanced state of mind.

THE HEALING MANTRA
RA MA DA SA SA SAY SO HUNG

Ra Ma Da Sa is like a rare diamond, which connects you with the pure healing energy of the Universe. You can instill the health trend in your consciousness by injecting this strong healing vibration into your mind. Then your actions and whole being will obey that thought. In order to change health troubles, we must alter the process of thought that brings the crystallization of consciousness into different forms of matter and action.

The healing vibrations of Ra Ma Da Sa help you develop the pattern of health. This particular recording by Rootlight, which is set to a healing classical tune, can purify the aura and consolidate your mental projection into a one-pointed positivity towards yourself and your health. Listening to it helps rebalance the entire auric circulation and gives you a sense of security that activates your self-healing capacities. A consistent listening or chanting practice becomes impressive enough to permeate the subconscious, which in turn automatically influences the conscious mind. Then it becomes a part of one's deep intuitional conviction.

Ra Ma Da Sa is called the *Shushmana Mantra*. It contains the eight sounds that stimulate the Kundalini to flow in the central channel of the spine and in the spiritual centers. This sound balances the five zones of the left and right hemispheres of the brain to activate the neutral mind. As this happens, the hypothalamus pulsates in rhythm with the divine gland, causing the pituitary master gland to tune the entire glandular system. Then the sympathetic, parasympathetic and active nervous systems match the timing of the glandular system. As a result, the muscular system and cells in the blood work in conjunction to receive this healing vibration, and the rebuilding process of one's health is triggered.

Mantra	Meaning
Raa	*Sun / the fire principle*
Maa	*Moon / the water principle*
Daa	*receiver of SAA / the earth principle*
Saa	*totality / the air principle*
Saa	*totality*
Say	*spirit, energy*
So	*manifestation*
Hung	*experience of Thou*

The first part of the mantra *(Ra Ma Da Sa)* expands toward heaven. By repeating the sound *Sa* as a turning point, it causes the spirit to descend from above into matter in order to animate and vitalize it with healing and life. In other words, the second part of the mantra *(Sa Say So Hung)* brings the healing qualities of the superior world back down to the earth. The last stanza of the Emerald Tablet from the great Hermes Trismegistus, which reveals the secret of healing and order in the material plane, is followed in this mantra. It reads, "Ascend with great sagacity from earth to heaven, and then again descend to earth, and unite together the powers of things superior and inferior. Thus you will obtain the glory of the whole world, and obscurity will fly away from you. The secret is adaptation, transforming one thing into another thing." *Ra Ma Da Sa Sa Say So Hung* transforms an imbalanced and unhealthy body into an harmonious, healthy one. As in the Star of David—a symbol of two interlaced triangles—this mantra interlinks spirit with matter.

After *Sa* comes *Say*, which is the totality of experience. *So* is the personal sense of identity. *Hung* is the infinite, vibrating and real. *Hung* suggests *Hu*, which is the life of God in every thing and every being. The *ng* causes the sound in *Hung* to stimulate the divine glands. The sound of the breath is *So Hung*. The inhale is *So* and the exhale is *Hung*. The two qualities of *So Hung* together mean "I am Thou." As you chant this mantra, you expand toward the infinite and merge back with the finite. Most people have forgotten that their essence is with the infinite, unlimited creative power of the cosmos.

A regular listening practice is not only good for practical, preventative self-healthcare, but will also aid in the assurance of a healthier life. It can help preserve the body and pave the way toward a positive mental projection. Chanting or listening to this mantra set to this classical tune will drive out depression and revibrate your life. It is timeless and can not be outdated. It has worked in the past, it works now, and it will work in the future. There is no time, no place, no space and no condition attached to this mantra. It burns the seed of disease. Use it everyday. Offer it to anyone. If you work with it, it will work for you. In moments of anxiety, despair, fear or worry, let it be your safeguard. It will give you a strong sense of your own centeredness.

TRIPLE MANTRA

Practical experience, as far as dealing with the world of duality, has proven Triple Mantra to excel in keeping adversity and misfortune away. This is one mantra you will definitely want to commit to memory, because it is a powerful tool for defense. Even if you don't do anything else for the day, chanting it for 11–31 minutes will act as protection against all negative forces on your daily path. All opposing vibrations, thoughts, words and actions will be stopped and neutralized. When a situation in your life becomes difficult and you are surrounded by adversity, just perfect this mantra through focused repetition, and you will create a divine heat that will burn the karma and allow God to shine through. By doing the triple mantra every morning, you will strengthen your magnetic field, so that no negativity can enter your aura and you will be protected on four sides. It is one of the most powerful defensive things with which you can surround yourself.

TRIPLE MANTRA	MEANING
Ad Guray Nameh	Hail to the Primal Light
Jugad Guray Nameh	Hail to the Light throughout the ages,
Sat Guray Nameh	Hail to the True Light
Siri Guru Devay Nameh	Hail to the Transparent Light
Ad Such	It was true in the beginning,
Jugad Such	True through the ages,
Hehbee Such	And true even now.
Nanaka O-See Bee Such	Nanak shall ever be true.
Ad Such	
Jugad Such	
Hehbeh Such	
Nanaka O-See Beh Such	

There are three parts to this mantra. The first part, starting with AD GURAY NAMEH, will surround you with a powerful light of protection. The first part of this mantra alone should be chanted as soon as you sit in a car or airplane to prevent accidents. Chanting this mantra gives you space, which means that your aura protects you by 9 feet. If you are early or late by 9 feet, you may not be entangled with that moment in time of a particular event. In other words, you cannot stop time, but you can gain or lose space. It is a sure protection against car, plane or other accidents. The second part of the mantra, starting with AD SUCH, will remove obstacles in your spiritual path. The third part will remove all types of obstacles in your daily life.

TIME

Chant aloud for 11 minutes, working up to 31. Take a minute or more of absolute silence and stillness to savor the experience.

One time in Trinidad, a friend was giving me a ride to the airport. It was early morning and still dark. I mentally vibrated the mantra. As soon as I was done, I realized that we were going 70 m.p.h., heading straight towards a gasoline truck stationed in the left portion of the road. I calmly asked my friend to move the car to the right. We barely avoided a serious accident. When we got to the airport, I had missed my plane. Luckily, the coordinator of the workshop I was to give was late to the airport as well. When he arrived, we arranged for a private plane to fly us over the water to Tobago Bay. Before the plane started, I whispered the triple mantra again with my hands in prayer pose. As soon as the plane moved, its wing crashed with another big plane, which was also on the ground. It turned out that our pilot and co-pilot were seriously drunk. We got out of that plane and waited four hours for another plane to take us safely to the hotel where I was scheduled to lecture. In these two particular cases, the triple mantra deflected something that could have been much more serious.

HEAVEN'S TOUCH
Guru Guru Wa-hey Guru
Guru Ram Das Guru

The first part of this mantra (*Guru Guru Wa-Hey Guru*) is called a *Nirgun* mantra, which vibrates to the cosmic, and projects the mind to the source of knowledge and ecstasy. The second part (*Guru Ram Das Guru*) is a *sirgun* mantra, which represents form and calls upon the wisdom that comes as a servant of the infinite. This mantra projects the mind to infinity so as to allow a guiding relationship to come into your practical activities. This is a mantra of humility that brings emergency saving grace and spiritual guiding light. This meditation can be done with your hands in prayer pose. Prayer pose neutralizes the energy flow within the body and keeps you centered.

The benefits of this mantra also encompass the healing and protective energy represented by Guru Ram Das who was known for universal service. This meditation brings protection and healing of any physical, mental or circumstantial situations. In the midst of trial and danger, this mantra can rescue you. It has a very soothing effect on the personality. This meditation brings the mind, body and spirit under control, and enables you to meditate on your own divine force, your own fiber. If the fiber of the being is not right, the being itself cannot be right. It is very important to be centered. When you are centered, you're not susceptible to upsetting and unsettled circumstances. This mantra will invoke and develop in you the values which will be unbeatable in the times to come. Guru Ram Das synchronizes your energies and hypnotizes your pituitary, which is your control center, so that it may serve your power of prayer.

On this particular recording by Rootlight, it is not by chance that this mantra is repeated five times per breath. The number five conceals the most profound arcana. All those captivated by the mystical and noble secret science will be familiar with the beauty and power of the mantra's rhythm. From the high science we know that five is the number of the Human that has fallen from his high estate because of disobedience to the laws of God. Five is also the number of the will, the instrument of reintegration. It can cause one to enter into his glory, assuming with him his regenerated human nature. Five is the great redemptive force of the will. For the full effect, try if you can, to do each of the five repetitions in one breath.

Sat Narayan Wa-hey Guru
Hari Narayan Sat Nam

This mantra creates internal peace allowing one to project outer peace. It gives one a clear perception of the truth. *Narayan* is the aspect of infinity that relates to water. *Hari Narayan* is creative sustenance which makes the one who chants it intuitively clear or healing. *Sat Narayan* is the true sustainer. *Wa-hey Guru* is indescribable wisdom. *Sat Nam* is true identity.

Never persuade yourself that you possess wisdom in virtue of mere memory or mere mental culture. Wisdom is like a mother's love, which makes itself felt only after the labours and pains of childbirth.

—Louis Claude St. Martin

Chapter Eighteen

Psalm 119

Psalm 119 is composed of the 22 prayers, representing the 22 letters of the Hebrew alphabet. The 22 letters are important, because they represent the 22 different levels of consciousness. They are the symbolic DNA of creation. They not only correspond to the 22 major arcana of the tarot cards, but also they represent cosmic forces.

Psalms are Kabbalah tools filled with immense power. In this particular Psalm, you are working with the energy that is contained within these words. They have been infused with light, therefore the power goes far beyond the mere meanings of the phrases. Much can be accomplished by working with these letters.

APPLICATIONS

Here are some of the ways of receiving light from the 22 prayers contained in Psalm 119.

1. If it is your birthday and you wish to give yourself a fresh start, so you may face your new year with renewed energy, read the whole Psalm.

2. If you know someone who is very ill and needs healing and light, have them read and meditate on the 22 prayers.

3. You may read the entire Psalm 119 on the four most powerful days of the year (Spring Equinox, Summer Solstice, Autumn Equinox, Winter Solstice) to completely revitalize your energies.

4. If you want to send light or healing energy to a loved one, keep him or her in mind as you recite these 22 levels of the cosmic force.

ALEPH (1)

Blessed are the undefiled in the way,
who walk in the law of the Lord.
Blessed are they that keep his testimonies,
and that seek him with the whole heart.
They also do no iniquity: they walk in his ways.
Thou hast commanded us to keep thy precepts diligently.
O that my ways were directed to keep thy statutes!
Then shall I not be ashamed when I have respect
unto all thy commandments.
I will praise thee with uprightness of heart,
when I shall have learned thy righteous judgments.
I will keep thy statutes: O forsake me not utterly.

BETH (2)

Wherewithal shall a young man cleanse his way?
by taking heed thereto according to thy word.
With my whole heart have I sought thee:
O let me not wander from thy commandments.
Thy word have I hid in mine heart,
that I might not sin against thee.
Blessed art thou, O Lord: teach me thy statutes.
With my lips have I declared all the judgments of thy mouth.
I have rejoiced in the way of thy testimonies,
as much as in all riches.
I will meditate in thy precepts, and have respect unto thy ways.
I will delight myself in thy statutes: I will not forget thy word.

GIMEL (3)

Deal bountifully with thy servant, that I may live,
and keep thy word.
Open thou mine eyes, that I may behold wondrous things
out of thy law.
I am a stranger in the earth: hide not thy commandments from me.
My soul breaketh for the longing that it hath
unto thy judgments at all times.
Thou has rebuked the proud that are cursed,
which do err from thy commandments.
Remove from me reproach and contempt;
for I have kept thy testimonies.
Princes also did sit and speak against me:
but thy servant did meditate in thy statutes.
Thy testimonies also are my delight and my counselors.

DALETH (4)

My soul cleaveth unto the dust: quicken thou me
according to thy word.
I have declared my ways, and thou heardest me:
teach me thy statutes.
Make me to understand the way of thy precepts:
so shall I talk of thy wondrous works.
My soul melteth for heaviness:
strengthen thou me according unto thy word.
Remove from me the way of lying:
and grant me thy law graciously.
I have chosen the way of truth:
thy judgments have I laid before me.
I have stuck unto thy testimonies: O Lord, put me not to shame.
I will run the way of thy commandments,
when thou shalt enlarge my heart.

HE (5)

Teach me, O Lord, the way of thy statutes;
and I shall keep it unto the end.
Give me understanding, and I shall keep thy law;
yea, I shall observe it with my whole heart.
Make me to go in the path of thy commandments;
for therein do I delight.
Incline my heart unto thy testimonies, and not to covetousness.
Turn away mine eyes from beholding vanity;
and quicken thou me in thy way.
Stablish thy word unto thy servant, who is devoted to thy fear.
Turn away my reproach which I fear: for thy judgments are good.
Behold, I have longed after thy precepts:
quicken me in thy righteousness.

VAU (6)

Let thy mercies come also unto me, O Lord, even thy salvation,
according to thy word.
So shall I have wherewith to answer him that reproacheth me:
for I trust in thy word.
And take not the word of truth utterly out of my mouth;
for I have hoped in thy judgments.
So shall I keep thy law continually for ever and ever.
And I will walk at liberty: for I seek thy precepts.
I will speak of thy testimonies also before kings,
and will not be ashamed.
And I will delight myself in thy commandments,
which I have loved.
My hands also will lift up unto thy commandments,
which I have loved;
and I will meditate in thy statutes.

ZAIN (7)

Remember the word unto thy servant,
upon which thou hast caused me to hope.
This is my comfort in my affliction:
for thy word hath quickened me.
The proud have had me greatly in derision:
yet have I not declined from thy law.
I remembered thy judgments of old, O Lord;
and have comforted myself.
Horror hath taken hold upon me
because of the wicked that forsake thy law.
Thy statutes have been my songs in the house of my pilgrimage.
I have remembered thy name, O Lord, in the night,
and have kept thy law.
This I had, because I kept thy precepts.

CHETH (8)

Thou art my portion, O Lord,
I have said that I would keep thy words.
I entreated thy favour with my whole heart:
be merciful unto me according to thy word.
I thought on my ways, and turned my feet unto thy testimonies.
I made haste, and delayed not to keep thy commandments.
The bands of the wicked have robbed me:
but I have not forgotten thy law.
At midnight I will rise to give thanks unto thee
because of thy righteous judgments.
I am a companion of all them that fear thee,
and of them that keep thy precepts.
The earth, O Lord, is full of thy mercy: teach me thy statutes.

TETH (9)

Thou hast dealt well with thy servant, O Lord,
according unto thy word.
Teach me good judgment and knowledge:
for I have believed thy commandments.
Before I was afflicted I went astray: but now have I kept thy word.
Thou art good, and doest good; teach me thy statutes.
The proud have forged a lie against me:
but I will keep thy precepts with my whole heart.
Their heart is as fat as grease, but I delight in thy law.
It is good for me that I have been afflicted;
that I might learn thy statutes.
The law of thy mouth is better unto me than
thousands of gold and silver.

JOD (10)

Thy hands have made me and fashioned me: give me understanding,
that I may learn thy commandments.
They that fear thee will be glad when they see me;
because I have hoped in thy word.
I know, O Lord, that thy judgments are right,
and that thou in faithfulness hast afflicted me.
Let, I pray thee, thy merciful kindness be for my comfort,
according to thy word unto thy servant.
Let thy tender mercies come unto me, that I may live:
for thy law is my delight.
Let the proud be ashamed; for they dealt perversely with me without a cause:
but I will meditate in thy precepts.
Let those that fear thee turn unto me,
and those that have known thy testimonies.
Let my heart be sound in thy statutes; that I be not ashamed.

CAPH (11)

My soul fainteth for thy salvation: but hope in thy word.
Mine eyes fail for thy word, saying, When wilt thou comfort me?
For I am become like a bottle in the smoke;
yet do I not forget thy statutes.
How many are the days of thy servant?
When wilt thou execute judgment on them that persecute me?
The proud have digged pits for me, which are not after thy law.
All thy commandments are faithful:
they persecute me wrongfully;
help thou me.
They had almost consumed me upon earth;
but I forsook not thy precepts.
Quicken me after thy lovingkindness;
so shall I keep the testimony of thy mouth.

LAMED (12)

For ever, O Lord, thy word is settled in heaven.
Thy faithfulness is unto all generations:
thou hast established the earth, and it abideth.
They continue this day according to thine ordinances;
for all are thy servants.
Unless thy law had been my delights,
I should then have perished in mine affliction.
I will never forget thy precepts:
for with them thou hast quickened me.
I am thine, save me; for I have sought thy precepts.
The wicked have waited for me to destroy me:
but I will consider thy testimonies.
I have seen an end of all perfection:
but thy commandment is exceeding broad.

MEM (13)

O how love I thy law! it is my meditation all the day.
Thou through thy commandments hast made me
wiser than mine enemies:
for they are ever with me.
I have more understanding than all my teachers:
for thy testimonies are my meditation.
I understand more than the ancients, because I keep thy precepts.
I have refrained my feet from every evil way,
that I might keep thy every word.
I have not departed from thy judgments: for thou hast taught me.
How sweet are thy words unto my taste!
yea, sweeter than honey to my mouth.
Through thy precepts I get understanding:
therefore I hate every false way.

NUN (14)

Thy word is a lamp unto my feet, and a light unto my path.
I have sworn, and I will perform it,
that I will keep thy righteous judgments.
I am afflicted very much: quicken me, O Lord,
according unto thy word.
Accept, I beseech thee, the freewill offerings of my mouth,
O Lord, and teach me thy judgments.
My soul is continually in my hand: yet do I not forget thy law.
The wicked have laid a snare for me:
yet I erred not from thy precepts.
Thy testimonies have I taken as an heritage for ever:
for they are the rejoicing of my heart.
I have inclined mine heart to perform thy statutes always,
even unto the end.

SAMECH (15)

I hate vain thoughts: but thy law do I love.
Thou art my hiding place and my shield: I hope in thy word.
Depart from me, ye evildoers:
for I will keep the commandments of my God.
Uphold me according unto thy word, that I may live:
and let me not be ashamed of my hope.
Hold thou me up, and I shall be safe:
and I will have respect unto thy statutes continually.
Thou hast trodden down all them that err from thy statutes:
for their deceit is falsehood.
Thou puttest away all the wicked of the earth like dross:
therefore I live thy testimonies.
My flesh trembleth for fear of thee;
and I am afraid of thy judgments.

AIN (16)

I have done judgment and justice: leave me not to mine oppressors.
Be surety for thy servant for good: let not the proud oppress me.
Mine eyes fail for thy salvation,
and for the word of thy righteousness.
Deal with thy servant according unto thy mercy,
and teach me thy statutes.
I am thy servant; give me understanding,
that I may know thy testimonies.
It is time for thee, Lord, to work: for they have made void thy law.
Therefore I love thy commandments above gold;
yea, above fine gold.
Therefore I esteem all thy precepts concerning
all things to be right;
and I hate every false way.

PE (17)

Thy testimonies are wonderful: therefore doth my soul keep them.
The entrance of thy words giveth light;
it giveth understanding unto the simple.
I opened my mouth, and panted:
for I longed for thy commandments.
Look thou upon me, and be merciful unto me,
as thou usest to do unto those that love thy name.
Order my steps in thy word:
and let not any iniquity have dominion over me.
Deliver me from the oppression of man: so will I keep thy precepts.
Make thy face to shine upon thy servant;
and teach me thy statutes.
Rivers of waters run down mine eyes,
because they keep not thy law.

TZADDI (18)

Righteous art thou, O Lord, and upright are thy judgments.
Thy testimonies that thou hast commanded
are righteous and very faithful.
My zeal hath consumed me, because mine enemies have
forgotten thy words.
Thy word is very pure: therefore thy servant loveth it.
I am small and despised: yet do not I forget thy precepts.
Thy righteousness is an everlasting righteousness,
and thy law is the truth.
Trouble and anguish have taken hold on me:
yet thy commandments are my delights.
The righteousness of thy testimonies is everlasting:
give me understanding, and I shall live.

KOPH (19)

I cried with my whole heart; hear me, O Lord:
I will keep thy statutes.
I cried unto thee; save me, and I shall keep thy testimonies.
I prevented the dawning of the morning, and cried:
I hoped in thy word.
Mine eyes prevent the night watches,
that I might meditate in thy word.
Hear my voice according unto thy lovingkindness:
O Lord, quicken me according to thy judgment.
They draw nigh that follow after mischief:
they are far from thy law.
Thou art near, O Lord; and all thy commandments are truth.
Concerning thy testimonies,
I have known of old that thou hast founded them for ever.

RESH (20)

Consider mine affliction, and deliver me:
for I do not forget thy law.
Plead my cause, and deliver me: quicken me according to thy word.
Salvation is far from the wicked: for they seek not thy statutes.
Great are thy tender mercies, O Lord:
quicken me according to thy judgments.
Many are my persecutors and mine enemies;
yet do I not decline from thy testimonies.
I beheld the transgressors, and was grieved;
because they kept not thy word.
Consider how I love thy precepts: quicken me,
O Lord, according to thy lovingkindness.
Thy word is true from the beginning:
and every one of thy righteous judgments endureth for ever.

SCHIN (21)

Princes have persecuted me without a cause:
but my heart standeth in awe of thy word.
I rejoice at thy word, as one that findeth great spoil.
I hate and abhor lying: but thy law do I love.
Seven times a day do I praise thee
because of thy righteous judgments.
Great peace have they which love thy law:
and nothing shall offend them.
Lord, I have hoped for thy salvation, and done thy commandments.
My soul hath kept thy testimonies; and I love them exceedingly.
I have kept thy precepts and thy testimonies:
for all my ways are before thee.

*TAU (22)

Let my cry come near before thee, O Lord:
give me understanding according to thy word.
Let my supplication come before thee:
deliver me according to thy word.
My lips shall utter praise, when thou hast taught me thy statutes.
My tongue shall speak of thy word:
for all thy commandments are righteousness.
Let thine hand help me; for I have chosen thy precepts.
I have longed for thy salvation, O Lord; and thy law is my delight.
Let my soul live, and it shall praise thee;
and let thy judgments help me.
I have gone astray like a lost sheep; seek thy servant;
for I do not forget thy commandments.

Conclusion

It has been such a blessing during my early years of spiritual exploration to be exposed to the traditional arcanas and be initiated
into many spiritual orders. Later, by the grace of God, I came in
touch with the teachings of Yogi Bhajan. Then all of my studies
from various sources came together.

The divine spiritual wisdom revealed in *Lifting the Veil* is designed
to expand our consciousness and facilitate our awakening into truth
and light, so that we may heal and empower ourselves and help
others do the same. Each person, like you and I, who walks the path
of light may use this spiritual wisdom to become a conduit through
which the light of the Sun may shine, so that we may uplift others
by spreading this healing energy through our presence, thoughts,
speech and actions.

The Seven Creative Planets direct and control the entire course
of life. These are the natural laws by which we must live in this age
in order to experience grace, harmony and self-protection in our
lives. This knowledge is either unknown or neglected by the average
person. By working with this knowledge, we can establish a healing
connection with our soul and start to see the unseen.

Humans, by nature, are imperfect. As a result, we make mistakes.
Most of those mistakes can be avoided if we are in harmony with
the Universe and use our intuition. Some mistakes in this age of
Light can have very costly repercussions. Therefore, I have presented
some basic, yet fundamental laws that have successfully passed the
test of time. Since many people, including myself, have proven the

accuracy of these principles, I am inspired to share them with my readers, so that we can all contribute to a positive evolution of humankind. Knowledge is power; it is light. By offering this book to someone, you are giving them light, for light is the highest gift one can give.

The wisdom of Kabbalah and Kundalini yoga are the birthright of all humankind, and as such, should be accessible to all. I have endeavored to make these principles so clear, that I trust you will comprehend the fundamental ideas and principles herein revealed, so we may all heal ourselves and help uplift the world.

The most humble on this earth plane are
the most high in the house of God.
The higher one goes on the spiritual path,
the more simple, humble, tolerant, compassionate
and non-judgmental one becomes.

True and genuine spiritual growth
expands a person, and one no longer has
the time nor inclination to criticize,
gossip and judge others.

Let the true servant of the Universe aim
at simplicity and tolerance, for the doorway to heaven
is so low that only little children along with humble,
simple and serviceful people can enter.
All spiritual powers acquired on the way,
must be redirected to heal the suffering of others,
and help the race evolve.

—Joseph Michael Levry (Gurunam)

About the Author

Joseph Michael Levry, also known by his spiritual name, Gurunam, is CEO and founder of Universal Force and CEO of Rootlight, Inc. He is also the founder of Universal Force Yoga and Healing Center located in New York City. He has spent 30 years studying, researching and teaching the sacred sciences of Kundalini yoga and Kabbalah.

He is a world-renowned Kabbalist, expert in Kundalini yoga, and the developer of Harmonyum, a transcendental healing system born out of Universal Kabbalah. One of his publications includes a complete correspondence course on the practical application of the sacred science of Kabbalah and Kundalini yoga in daily life.

Since the age of 12, Joseph Michael Levry has been trained in the esoteric arts and sciences and initiated into many spiritual orders, through which he learned the science of Kabbalah. He has, in his books and lectures, illuminated the symbols of Kabbalah that were once kept secret within the doctrines of Judaism, Christianity and many other religions. Time and time again, he has earned the trust of even the most skeptical by his precise diagnosis of physical ailments, through his well-known unique ability to see and analyze the energy field.

After 25 years of study, research, teaching and travel worldwide, he has created a unique synthesis of the most powerful teachings of Kabbalah and Kundalini yoga, to not only uplift people, but also to help them avoid adversity and improve their lives. He believes that nothing is done by chance, and one can rewrite his or her destiny through the knowledge and application of this divine spiritual wisdom.

Joseph Michael Levry, who resides in New York City, also holds a Master of Science degree in Industrial Engineering. He currently travels nine months of each year, lecturing throughout the world, focusing on New York, Los Angeles, Sweden, Germany, the UK and France. He corresponds with thousands of people of every race and religion, guiding them through the process of self-healing, creating meaningful careers, healthy relationships and realizing their dreams.

HEALING BEYOND MEDICINE SERIES

To obtain our full, updated list of publications and offerings, such as books and meditation/mantra CDs, please contact Rootlight, Inc, by phone, mail, e-mail or web site. In addition, contact us if you would like more information on Gurunam's Practical Kabbalah Workshops, Kundalini yoga and Meditation Intensives or Harmonyum Healing.

Other Books:
The Splendor of the Sun: Mastering the Invisible Sunlight Fluid for Healing and Spiritual Growth

This book will show you practical ways of connecting with the Sun in order to capture its many benefits and blessings. Working with the Sun is one of the highest, most potent and effective spiritual systems you can come across on this earth. Working with the Sun will cause your soul to become active and your spiritual powers to become operative, showing clear visible signs in your mind, spirit and physical body. On a physical level, working with the Sun sparks a complete metamorphosis and renewal of the cells and tissues in the body—all the unhealthy cells and energies are replaced, resulting in health, vitality, complete balance and intelligence.

Alchemy of Love Relationships

A practical guide to successful relationships through the application of spiritual principles from Kabbalah and Kundalini yoga. The application of these principles will completely change your approach to life and relationships. This is an invaluable book for a richer and more fulfilling love relationship.

Correspondence Course (Levels 1–3)
The Sacred Teachings of Kabbalah with Kundalini Yoga

Kabbalah and Kundalini yoga are two ancient and powerful sciences for spiritual growth, and for understanding one's self in relation to the Universe. This course is a compelling and extremely practical masterpiece of Universal Kabbalah. The sacred teachings of Kabbalah have been presented in a practical, doable and understandable way. You will be given some of the most effective meditations and prayers that Kabbalah and Kundalini Yoga have to offer. The essence of Kabbalah, that was previously hidden and confusingly presented in various books, has been decoded and put into a form that is effective and powerful in its application. By working with this course, all the dormant qualities and virtues in you are brought to full life, resulting in improved health and well-being on all levels. Then your spiritual knowledge, presence and words will start healing and uplifting others.

CDs

BLISSFUL SPIRIT — Wahe Guru/Har Har Gobinday/Ganputi Mantra
These sound vibrations eliminate mental impurities and cause the spirit to blossom, while bestowing divine grace and radiance.

GREEN HOUSE — Har Har Gobinday (II)/Har Haray Haree (I, II)
These sound vibrations extend the power of projection and protection in the personality. They help open the door to opportunities and attract blessings.

HEALING FIRE — Ong/Prayer of Light/12 seed sounds
These sound vibrations give youth, beauty and spiritual illumination. They work on the glandular system and organs. A regular practice of listening to this CD or chanting along with it promotes good health and helps develop intuitive intelligence.

HEAVEN'S TOUCH — Guru Ram Das/Sat Narayan
These sound vibrations bring grace, blessings and internal peace. The sound current on the first track synchronizes your energy and expands the aura. It is also for emergency saving grace and spiritual guiding light. The second sound current cleanses the emotions, creates internal peace and allows you to project outer peace. The third track moves you into a meditative space with rhythm.

LUMEN DE LUMINE—For opening the heart and touching the soul
This sound vibration surrounds those who chant or listen to it with a blanket of light. Just listen to it and it will purify and strengthen your aura. Play it in a room and it will clear the energy in a short time. Go to sleep with it and you will wake up revitalized. When faced with challenges, play it continuously; it will eat the darkness out of your life.

RA MA DA SA—To heal and/or maintain balance and health
This sound vibration cuts across time and space and brings healing. It maintains, strengthens and improves your health. It can generate beneficial energy in hospital rooms and places of recovery. It will also create a peaceful and productive environment in the workplace. Families can benefit from its harmonizing effects on the home, children and even pets.

SOUL TRANCE — Wahe Guru (II)/Har/Peace, Light, Love to All
These sound vibrations help awaken the soul, so you may manifest your higher destiny. They help give clarity, stability, and harmony.

TRIPLE MANTRA—For protection and to clear obstacles
This sound vibration clears all types of psychic and physical obstacles in one's daily life. It will strengthen your magnetic field and keep negativity away, and it is a powerful protection against car, plane or other accidents. This mantra cuts through all opposing vibrations, thoughts, words and actions.

Please visit us at www.rootlight.com for more selections

Rootlight Order Form

Title	Each	Qty.	Subtotal
Books			
Alchemy of Love Relationships	$23	x _____ =	_____
Lifting the Veil	$23	x _____ =	_____
Spendor of the Sun	$23	x _____ =	_____
Correspondence Course			
Level 1	$360	x _____ =	_____
Level 2	$360	x _____ =	_____
Level 3	$360	x _____ =	_____
CDs			
Blissful Spirit	$19	x _____ =	_____
Green House	$19	x _____ =	_____
Healing Fire	$19	x _____ =	_____
Heaven's Touch	$19	x _____ =	_____
Lumen de Lumine	$19	x _____ =	_____
OM House	$19	x _____ =	_____
Ra Ma Da Sa	$19	x _____ =	_____
Soul Trance	$19	x _____ =	_____
Triple Mantra	$19	x _____ =	_____

Shipping in USA:
add $5.50 for 1st item,
$.50 each additional item.

SUBTOTAL _____
Shipping/Handling _____
N.Y. Residents add 8.25% tax _____
TOTAL DUE _____

PLEASE CONTINUE ORDER ON OTHER SIDE OF FORM ➡

Prices subject to change. (03/03)

(Please Print Clearly)

PAYMENT INFORMATION:

Payment enclosed: ❏ Check   ❏ Money Order
Please make checks payable to Rootlight, Inc.

Please charge order to my Credit Card: ❏ Visa ❏ Mastercard

NAME AS SHOWN ON CARD: _____

CREDIT CARD NUMBER _____

EXPIRATION DATE MM/DD/YYYY _____

SIGNATURE _____

SHIPPING INFORMATION

NAME _____

ADDRESS _____

CITY _____ STATE _____ ZIP _____

PHONE OR E-MAIL (if we have questions about your order) _____

Thank you for your order!
Please also visit us at www.rootlight.com

ROOTLIGHT, INC.
15 Park Avenue Suite 7C
New York, NY 10016
T: (212) 769-8115
rootlight@earthlink.net
rootlightorder@aol.com